351-

Ancient Peoples and Places

THE
VIKINGS

General Editor
DR GLYN DANIEL

Ancient Peoples and Places

THE
VIKINGS

Holger Arbman

Translated and edited with
an introduction by
Alan Binns

67 PHOTOGRAPHS
38 LINE DRAWINGS
AND 6 MAPS

London
THAMES AND HUDSON

THIS IS VOLUME TWENTY-ONE IN THE SERIES

Ancient Peoples and Places

GENERAL EDITOR: DR GLYN DANIEL

© THAMES AND HUDSON LONDON 1961
NEW EDITION 1962
PRINTED IN GREAT BRITAIN
BY WESTERN PRINTING SERVICES LTD BRISTOL
NOT TO BE IMPORTED FOR SALE INTO THE USA

CONTENTS

ILLUSTRATIONS

Introduction

I T MAY BE that the strength of the emotions which the impact of the Vikings on Western Europe once aroused still
affects consideration of them. They have been seen in the somewhat lurid light thrown upon them by the ecclesiastical chroniclers who were their victims, as fierce pirates preying upon
civilization. Accepting this view, later writers have usually
condemned them out of hand, though some (evidently envying
them their opportunities) have sentimentalized upon their boldness and independence. The first school is unwilling to allow
them any importance in the history of European culture other
than that of a cataclysm from which Europe eventually recovered: the second, by regarding them as Tacitus regarded the
ancient inhabitants of Germania, or Rousseau his noble savage,
leaves out of account the possibility of their having contributed
to European civilization anything in return for what they took
from it. It sometimes seems that the Viking expeditions are
construed by both schools as an adventurous but uncompli-
cated saga of the burning of monastic libraries and the destruc-
tion of bookish culture, and given the blame (or praise)
accordingly. Yet King Alfred, who was in a good position to
judge, was conscientious enough to observe that the libraries of
which England was full 'before it was all harried and pillaged'
were losing their utility, as learning had completely declined
before the Viking raids which some modern historians have
alleged as the excuse.

It is natural that we should think of the Vikings in the ships
which were their greatest masterpieces, armed with axe and
sword raiding some exposed shore, for it was this which they
celebrated in their own literature. But it would be wrong to
suppose that their society was less complex than the hieratic,

traditional and highly local one which they disturbed. Wulfstan of York, in his sermon to the English 'when they were most persecuted by the Danes', finds it particularly unnatural that 'Should a serf escape from his lord and turn from Christianity to the Vikings, if he meets his former lord in a fight and kills him, he does not need to pay *wergild* to his lord's relatives; and if his lord should kill him, he will have to pay *wergild* for him as if he had been a free man.' The greater proportion of free men in the Danelaw than in the rest of England at the Domesday survey suggests that the characteristic of the culture of the Vikings (at any rate in their impact on others) was a mobility not only geographic but social. Their achievements in ship-building, navigation and trade may seem to amount to a technology rather than a civilization, and the typical empiricism of *Hávamal*

> The coward thinks he will live for ever
> If only he keeps clear of fights
> But old age will give him no truce
> Even if weapons do.

or

> In the evening can the day be praised
> And when she's dead a wife
> A sword when you have made trial of it
> A maiden when she's married
> Praise ice when you've got over it
> And beer when it's drunk.

may not seem very inspiring, may seem inappropriate to the heroic Viking. One has to substitute for the heroic Viking drinking mead from the skulls of his enemies in Valhalla (the result of an unfortunate eighteenth-century mistranslation of a poetic phrase for 'drinking horn') the accomplished technologist moving restlessly from one country to another, his main principle that things can be judged only in the light of actual experience, and prepared to sell his services to the highest bidder. This figure is perhaps no more truly representative than the bloodthirsty pirate or noble savage of previous generations, and he may seem even less attractive; but he could not be called irrelevant to our developed civilization, and the merits of his art, its rhythm and strength and firm acceptance of the limita- tions of the raw material being worked may be more apparent to us than to our predecessors.

Of the first importance for the understanding of a technolo- gist are the tools of his trade, and there, in the case of the Vikings, were ships and weapons. The ships are well known to us through the accident of their preservation, hermetically sealed in the blue clay of the Norwegian burial mounds of Tune, Gokstad and Oseberg: models and copies of varying accuracy have spread the image of these vessels as the typical Viking war-galley. They are not the vessels which actually carried the Vikings to foreign shores. A facsimile of the Gokstad ship crossed the Atlantic under sail in 1893, but though this shows that such ships could have been used for the voyages to Iceland, Greenland and America, it does not prove that they were. On warlike expeditions the fighting men could work their passage by pulling at the oars, but long passages laden with cargo must have relied upon sail in the main, with smaller crews (between 15 and 30 men) to pay and feed. It is clear from the account of their voyages that Ohthere and Wulfstan gave to King Alfred that their vessels were propelled by sail and not oars. Though no such vessels have survived, we know something of the way in which they were navigated, and some features of the Gokstad ship can give us a good idea of their actual construction. The Oseberg ship on the other hand, whilst it has much to tell us about Viking art, would never have been chosen by the most reckless Viking for a sea passage. Its mast-step was split (and had been repaired with an iron band) when it was buried, and seems ludicrously weak for its job, even on a vessel which because of its lack of ballast would

Plate 20

not stand up to the wind and so put much strain on the mast.

The Gokstad ship is 76½ feet over-all, with a beam of 17 feet, a hull draught of under 3 feet (the rudder projected below this) and a freeboard amidships of 3 feet 9 inches. These dimen-sions must increase one's admiration for the crew under Cap-tain Magnus Andersen which took such a vessel across the Atlantic, but the capacity of such a vessel in modern measure-ment is only just over 30 tons register, and it is clear that the use of oars for propulsion has influenced the design. The oars are by no means the heavy sweeps with a long and ponderous stroke that some have imagined. They are only 16 feet long (through at bow and stern, where the bulwark was higher above the waterline, they are longer in compensation), no longer than modern lifeboat oars, and are light and very narrow-bladed. Recent experience with teams of trained rowers in facsimile vessels has shown that the stroke required is the short quick one needed for rowing at sea as distinct from racing on rivers. We may be sure that any vessel relying more on sail had a greater draft and freeboard, and for economic reasons a greater capa-city. They need not for this reason have been clumsy, for the Gokstad ship, with its keel a foot deeper amidships than at the ends, shows that the Viking naval architects knew how to make a vessel easily tacked by concentrating its lateral resistance amid-ships. The later story of Thorberg skavhogg (who damaged beyond repair by a blow from his axe a ship's sheer-line which he considered unsatisfactory) shows that there were recognized independent specialists in the art of naval architecture. It is not too much to say that it is this scientific approach to the ship's keel which made it possible for ships to sail across, or even close to the wind, as a vessel with a crew too few to row her had to do. The bottom planking of the Gokstad ship is only 1 inch thick, less than that of many modern vessels a quarter of her size, and shows a similar scientific confidence. Had it been bolted to the frames it would have had to be much thicker, otherwise the fastenings would have parted as it gave to the impact of the waves. The planks are carefully formed from wood originally three times as thick, so that on each side of each rib projecting pieces of the plank are tied (with flexible pine roots) through the rib. In this way maximum strength and watertightness are combined with minimum weight (and there-fore maximum performance) in a way reminiscent of the most technically refined modern racing machines, with a finesse that has not been equalled until our own century. The mast is stepped in a keel-block over 10 feet long to distribute the stress, and passes through an even longer beam (16 feet long) above the floors, with a hole which is lengthened in a fore and aft direction so that the mast can be easily raised and lowered. Abreast of its forward end each bulwark has fastened to its inner side a heavy beam with two holes which both point slightly upwards at different angles. These were presumably to take the end of the *beiti-áss*, the spar which was used to extend the foot of the otherwise loose-footed sail to make it possible to set up the sail's leading edge tightly enough to sail to windward. This spar must have been even more necessary in the *hafskip*, or ocean-going vessel without a full crew of rowers, and its proper management must have been the special concern of the sailing-master.

Thorsteinn Ox-leg, on King Olaf's Long Serpent at the battle of Svoldr, was rebuked by the king for not fighting respectably with sword and spear as God intended; he used his fists and then this spar to knock the enemy into the sea and his comment 'each man must do what he can' (i.e. knows how to) is a pleasant indication of the pride in the tools of his trade of the professional Viking seaman. It was the intelligent use of this device which freed the navigator from the necessity of awaiting a dead stern wind to blow him on his way, and for this among other reasons we may think that Ohthere, when he told King Alfred that at the North Cape of Norway he waited for the wind to go round to North of West before sailing further, was not confessing his utter dependence upon it. Later in his voyage he says he had to wait for a true stern wind to enter the White Sea, and this is understandable because of the strong stream of melting snow water which runs out of it: against such a stream he could not afford anything less than full speed ahead through the water with no leeway. The wait at North Cape has no hint of reluctance but rather of confidence, of a man expecting a natural development, as indeed he was. To double North Cape it was desirable to arrive as did Ohthere on the south-westerly winds of a depression which would blow him round against the prevailing north-easters, but also desirable to ensure that once there he did not lie in the path of the oncoming storm winds increasing in strength. His waiting until the wind shifted to North of West may well have been because he knew that the winds flow anti-clockwise around such systems, and that such a shift of wind indicated that the storm centre was safely past him to the north. Trawler skippers with great experience of the area at the present day share this view, that once the wind has gone North of West it will not freshen, and Ohthere's waiting for the change (which would not take long) was perhaps prudent rather than obligatory. The speed of his passage would not have been undeserving of comment even by nineteenth-century standards, and some apparent inconsistencies detected by editors in his account disappear when one adds in the allowances for the currents which are described in the modern pilot book. His day's run (corrected for current) then agrees very well indeed with the traditional 'day's sailing' of the sagas, 100 miles at 4 knots. Modern versions of the Gokstad ship with trained rowers have shown that it could have far exceeded this figure and the 1893 copy averaged 11 knots under sail on one day, but it is significant of the relative importance of the two types of ship that Ohthere's should have provided the norm for such expressions.

Two features which are most accepted as typical of the Viking ship are the row of shields along the bulwark and the rudder hung on the starboard (or steer-board) side and not at the stern; all models, however bad, show them. The first was probably merely a means of indicating the owner's prestige in harbour; they could scarcely be carried at sea, whether under oars or sail, when they would have greatly hampered the work- ing of the ship, and served no useful purpose. Indeed we know, as Shetelig has pointed out, that it was not done to carry them except in harbour, and an Icelander who sailed up the fjord with shields rigged received the nickname 'Shield-Björn' in consequence. The second feature, on the other hand, the rud- der, though strange to our eyes, was one of the best instances of the perfectly functional design of the ships. By its projection below the keel it served the purpose of a modern centre-board or lee-board in increasing the lateral resistance, and so the sailing efficiency, of the hull, and was easily raised to diminish the draught when the craft was beached. Its absence from the stern made possible the latter's graceful rising swell which kept the vessel dry when running before a following sea.

The sail of the Gokstad ship probably had red and white vertical stripes, but the carvings on the Gotland stones show a chequered pattern of intersecting diagonal lines, and we know Plate 21 from the literary sources also that this was used. The complicated network between sail and hull on some stones has sometimes been interpreted as a decorative extension of this in the tradi- tional interlace, but in the absence of free-running pulleys such a large sail must have been difficult to lower (we know that it was usually 'ridden down' by members of the crew astride it), particularly when filled by the wind. It seems likely that what is represented on the stones is a network of brailing lines which besides making it possible to furl up the sail to the yard, would support the loosely woven cloth of the sail, and prevent its distortion.

The magnetic compass was unknown, but it has been urged by C. V. Sølver that some form of sun-compass was used. The evidence which is claimed to support this is extremely dubious, but it is clear from the use of '*eyktarstaðr*' (S 60° W) in the description of Vinland's position that the Vikings had not only an understanding of the connection between the sun's amplitude and altitude and a given latitude, but also some means of establishing the azimuth corresponding to '*eyk-tarstaðr*' without reference to familiar landmarks. As some sort of bearing-dial or pelorus would be required for this, we may leave aside the question of whether the object excavated at Eystribygth in Greenland by C. L. Vebaek actually is such a dial, and say simply that some such device was used. It also seems likely that a rudimentary form of plot of distances and courses run was kept on the perforated 'gaming boards' reminiscent of the medieval traverse board on which a peg was moved the appropriate number of holes to register the distance sailed in various directions in the course of a day.

The axe has become accepted as the typical Viking weapon, and was evidently so accepted in the fourteenth century when the 'bearded' axe with its cutting edge extending downwards was called a Danes' axe. It is a Scandinavian type which was in its most characteristic form with the 'beard' most clearly marked, in the second half of the ninth century, and the survival of the type-name over five centuries of changing fashion into the fourteenth century suggests what a deep impression it had made. It was supplanted as the characteristic form of the tenth century by the more symmetrical type (with the blade slightly extended both upwards and downwards) which is found decorated in the Jellinge style. By A.D. 1000 the standard Viking battle-axe in use in the West seems to have had a graceful flare (unbroken by any beard or angle) from a narrow blade at the shaft to a broad curved blade, equally balanced above and below the point of junction with the shaft. This type is known from the area of the campaigns of Svein and Canute (those from the bed of the Thames near Old London Bridge, and the grapnel irons found with them, are presumably associated with Olaf's attack on the bridge described in *Olafs saga helga*); it is not as widely distributed as its predecessors with angular lower edges, which crop up from Orkney and Islay, Dublin and York over the whole area of Viking activity.

Some idea of the development of the sword can be gained from a similar contrast of distribution. In the Scottish Isles we find a simple straight-line 'cocked-hat' pommel with a straight hand-guard, which is evidently that used by the Norwegian settlers of the eighth and ninth centuries. A later type, of the first half of the tenth century, is found in a broad band from the Isle of Man across the Danelaw to Norwich. It has a high central tip to the cocked-hat pommel, and the guards are curved: examples of it found in Norway are decorated in English styles of ornament and it probably developed in the Viking kingdom of the British Isles, perhaps at the same time as the types more common on the Continent but rare in Britain. These had straight hand-guards and the cocked-hat sprouted into three or five lobes, the end lobes often taking the form of animal heads. The nearest example to these in Britain are the swords with roughly semicircular pommels divided into three sections by shallow grooves which are perhaps illustrated on some of the York Viking coins and on the Nunburnholme Stone near York. Two such swords have in fact been found in York, and some similar ones in Ireland taken together with them indicate the extent to which York, lying on the main Viking East-West route of communication, was more likely to be in touch with cosmopolitan taste than the other parts of Britain.

The sword type which corresponds in distribution to the battle-axes from the Thames is one which is also found in the river bed and is also absent from the Viking colonies in Ireland

and Scotland, though it is typical of the south and east of the Baltic. It is presumably that of the late tenth-century Vikings of Svein and Canute, and has three lobes and lightly curving guards; it can be seen worn by Canute himself in the drawing of him in the New Minster Register (MS Stowe 944).

The most important part of a sword, however, is not the ornamental features of the handle but the blade: and in many Viking swords these, like the handle, seem to have been imported, though probably from the workshops of the Rhine rather than the British Isles. Not all the blades stamped Ingelri or Ulfberht came from those famous makers, but it is clear that in many cases the blade was imported and then fitted with a handle to suit the local taste, whether that was English or Scandinavian. The main adornment of the blade was damascening, the wavy pattern reminiscent of an adder's back that may well have inspired the frequent references to 'serpent-patterned blades' in the literature of the period. Aslak Liestøl has shown reason to believe that Erik Blood-axe in York must have had a sword of this type, if his interpretation of a line in a poem of Egill in praise of Erik is correct. He has provided the most convincing explanation of the technique involved in the production of such pattern welded swords. Cross-sections of damascened swords show that some, like seaside rock, are 'lettered all through' which would not be the case if the older view (that the pattern was produced by beating strips of metal into grooves etched in the surface) were correct. Liestøl suggests that the process of manufacture was very similar to that involved in the production of a stick of patterned candy. The flat billet from which the sword was to be made was first laminated from two or three different steels, and then cut longitudinally into strips approximately square in section. These were twisted in various directions and then split in half. The sections along the axis of the bar thus revealed showed the irregular wavy pattern formed by the convoluted strata of the original laminated billet, and formed the outer surfaces of the new billet formed when the half-strips were again forged together. The patterns of damascening actually found in Viking swords of this kind can all be generated by the correct choice of: number of laminations of the original billet, number of rods it is cut into, direction of twisting applied to these rods, and plane (whether above or on the long axis of the rod) of section used to produce the surfaces used as outers. This technique is laborious and complicated (Liestøl analysed the blade of one sword thus formed to consist of 58 originally separate pieces!) but straightforward enough once understood, and probably within the capacity of Scandinavian smiths of the Viking period.

Arabic writers such as Al-Biruni and Al-Kindi cited by Professor Validi appear to credit two foreign peoples, the Franks and the Rus (or Swedish settlers in Russia), with the ability to make, or perhaps rather the habit of using, swords of laminations of soft iron and steel which are better in very cold conditions than those of Near Eastern steel (which has a different name). Aarvik's analysis of a sword of this type showed that the alternate laminates were of steel with 0·20 per cent carbon content and thinner ones of carbon-free steel, and the close alliance between function and ornament typical of the best design thus appears perhaps even in the damascening.

The shields and mail-shirts of the Bayeux Tapestry are not typical of the early Viking centuries; the pointed shield and very long mail-shirt have replaced the earlier round shield and short byrnie found in the pictures of warriors on the Middleton stones, though those suggest that a close-fitting pointed helmet with nose and cheek guards was being used by Vikings in the West already at the beginning of the tenth century. The more elaborate helmet descended from the type seen at Vendel or Sutton Hoo presumably survived, and is evidently indicated on some stones (e.g. Nunburnholme) but cannot have been part

Plate 25

of the equipment of every warrior, which was completed by a spear and a short one-edged knife, or *sax*, often with a very characteristic angle behind the point.

The heroic sagas of the Norsemen have played a part second only to their ships in the popular imagination. In the translations of William Morris and Sir George Dasent they confirmed the change from rapacious cruelty to noble resolution as the characteristic of 'our Scandinavian forebears', as the Vikings had begun to be called. W. P. Ker expresses the distinction very well when he tries to explain the anomaly that the blood-thirsty ruffian abroad should be the cultivated country gentle-man at home. We must remember that the best sagas are the work of contemporaries of Chaucer, three centuries after the end of the Viking Age. There is no reason to doubt that they are based upon a consciously cultivated tradition of oral history, whose continuance from the early Viking period can tell us much about the people concerned, but it would be danger-ous to assume that the events or principles asserted are true of the Viking Age. What Ker says of the sagas, 'the record of all this anarchy is a prose history, rational and unaffected, seeing all things in a dry light: a kind of literature that has not much to learn from any humanism or rationalism', is true enough of them and their authors, but we must not be misled into attribu-ting this clarity to all the first narrators who in the tenth century told for example of Egil's visit to York, any more than we should attribute the merits of Shakespeare's *Hamlet* or *Macbeth* to Holinshed or to tenth-century lost English sagas.

The gloomy empiricism of *Hávamal* is more at home in the Viking period than the already slightly formalized heroism of saga-heroes such as Gunnlaug or Gunnar, which because it was itself the work of later admirers of the Viking Age was so congenial to the nineteenth-century translators. The oral tradi-tion which the saga authors took as raw material originated in the Viking period, and from it we can see what captured the popular imagination, but the literature of the Viking period is represented in the sagas only by the skaldic verses quoted by the authors because they were accepted as being contemporary with the events described. These verses do not seem surprising as the product of the age. Their strong point is not any great subtlety or refinement of concept, for the ideas are usually simple—delight in a gift or good ship, flattery of a prince, rueful assess-ment of danger—and the effort has gone into technical com-plexities of expression, a sort of witty neatness rather than grace. Analogies between literature and the plastic arts are dangerous, but the distortion of normal syntax and fanciful elaboration of elements of minor significance provide in the skaldic poetry a parallel to the distortion of the animal for patterning purposes in Viking art. When Harald Hardrade at the head of the last Viking inroad before Stamford Bridge says:

> On we go in battle line
> Unarmoured against bright blades
> Helmets shine but I haven't mine
> All our mail-shirts are down at the ships

and then immediately apologizes for his inadequacy, saying 'That was no good, and I'll make a better poem', and substi-tutes

> We creep not up to weapons' crash
> The hawks' land's goddess bad me so;
> High, where battle-ice and helmet meet
> Amid the weapons din, my head to bear
> So bad the necklace-bearer fair

one feels that one has learnt something about the attitude to literature involved. The arm is the hawk's land, for the falcon was carried on it, and the fire of the arm is gold in the form of rings; so goddess of the fire of the hawks' land is a kenning for lady, compressed by the omission of 'fire'. Literature for the

Vikings evidently included the tragic lays of the Volsungs and various poems, both tragic and robustly farcical, about the Gods. For the rest they had elegant and highly professional occasional poetry which must seem to a modern reader deficient in feeling when it is compared with the contemporary poetry of for example the Anglo-Saxons. Only in some of the sea poetry does one capture a sense of real liveliness as well as contrivance.

If we would do well to be cautious in our use of the sagas as evidence for the literary taste (or events) of the Viking Age, we may be able to learn much from the contacts between Old Norse literature and other literatures in the period. The poets we know to have worked in the British Isles for the Viking rulers there can be distinguished from others by their richer style and use of rhyme, and it seems likely that they profited from the Latin verse cultivated in Anglo-Saxon England. The assonance and verse forms and expressions of skaldic poetry were derived from those of the Irish professional poets, according to Professor Turville-Petre, and the acceptance over the whole of Scandinavia of a literary style created by Norse artists from Irish and English elements in an English environment is bound to remind one of the origin of some decorative styles in Viking art. The other side of this contact is to be seen in the preservation by the chroniclers of the Church of the sort of material which in Iceland was used by later authors as the basis of sagas. There are good grounds for assuming that the cultural apparatus of the archdiocese of York was at the service of the Vikings.

The complicated history of events between the invasion of the Great Army of 867 and the death of Erik Blood-axe will eventually be established largely from the accomplished coinage produced by the ecclesiastical moneyers for their new masters, whereas the Five Boroughs, lacking the resources of York, are likely to remain unknown. The later Church historians are not necessarily giving us merely oral traditions of the Viking king-doms, though that would be valuable enough. There was evidently a written chronicle kept at York throughout its occu-pation, which accepted, at any rate partially, the Scandinavian view, and describes events as they affected their interests, in contrast to the other foreign chroniclers who viewed the Vikings as enemies. It does not survive, of course, but its existence may be reasonably inferred from the number of accounts of the history of the period from a Scandinavian point of view which appear in Church writers of the North of England and evi-dently share a common written source. Some indication of the sort of accommodation involved is to be seen in the manuscript of the Anglo-Saxon Chronicle which was derived from one kept in York: it omits the great Scandinavian defeat of Brunan-burh (the battle of Vinheiði in *Egilssaga*) but has an entry reminiscent of the interest in feud of the family sagas: 'In this year Sitric killed his brother Njal in Ireland.'

There are obvious dangers in building too much upon the interpretation of literary sources, which are in any case not available in anything approaching a contemporary form for Scandinavia itself in the Viking Age. But their intelligent and cautious use enables us at any rate to guess at the ideas and ambitions of the men involved in a movement that otherwise tends to be seen as an incomprehensible explosion of human energy which in the course of three centuries dissipated itself over the seas of the known world, leaving behind a few place-names and dialect words, and heroic stories whose point of view is so consistent as to give us the impression of an easily recognized individuality.

ALAN L. BINNS

Chapter I

The Background in Scandinavia

A NEW CULTURE is usually a gradual development, but in some circumstances very wide-ranging changes can happen very quickly without our being able to tell what the decisive factors were. Contacts with foreign countries are important, but rarely alone decisive. The Viking Age in Scandinavia may seem at first to have been a period of such sudden change, but a closer study of the archaeological material shows that a fundamental continuity underlies it. A gradual development in contact with Western Europe was already taking place in the preceding period, the Vendel age, indicated by the boat graves near Vendel church in Uppland in mid-Sweden. In these as in other boat-graves the dead were buried with food and weapons, and goods which already included glass beakers and woollen cloth from Western Europe.

The large farm on Helgö in Lake Mälaren, about 12 miles from Stockholm, was in close contact with Western Europe already in the eighth century, and its owners were evidently trading voyagers as well as farmers. The animal ornament found on grave goods of the period in Scandinavia also shows a connection with Western Europe, and reflects on small metal objects an art in wood now lost; but a better guide to the ideas of the period (for which we have no literary records) is the pictorial carving on the Gotland stones, particularly the eighth-century ones. Here we find Valhalla, and scenes from the Niebelung legend reminiscent of the Icelandic sagas and skalds associated with the Viking period; as no contemporary Scandinavian poem survives, the Old English *Beowulf*, with its rich material on Scandinavia, is our only comparable source.

One thing the archaeological material from the Vendel period does show clearly: the earlier occasional contacts with

Plates 1, 22

the other Baltic lands were soon succeeded by colonization. At Grobin, east of Libau in Courland (in Latvia) Birger Ner-man has, since 1929, excavated three separate burial fields ex-tending from about A.D. 650 to 800. In one, containing rem-nants of about a thousand cremations, both weapons and brooches were of characteristic Gotland patterns. One of the other two burial fields shared these features, but the third was quite different. Its graves were covered by mounds, and the grave goods show that there was a connection with the Mälar valleys of mid-Sweden. By Grobin there is a large fort with earthen ramparts, and from it come arrowheads and pottery of Mälar type. Grobin is probably the 'Seeburg' of the seven thou-sand warriors of Rimbert's life of St Ansgar, and the Apulia of the same text lies further south in Courland (now Apuole in north-western Lithuania) where one of the Baltic's largest old forts is found. It is even possible that the multitude of arrow-heads in the rampart is a relic of the Swedish capture.

Another Gotland colony on the south coast of the Baltic was near Elbing, perhaps the Truso described by Wulfstan to King Alfred. Graves furnished after Gotland's fashion there extend from the eighth century until well into the Viking Age.

We know nothing of the men who accomplished all this, in spite of the confused tales of Harald Hilditonn and Sigurd Hring in later sagas. It is only in the subsequent Viking period that written sources become available, and even then, in spite of Rimbert, Ohthere, and Wulfstan, for evidence on Scandi-navia we are almost confined to strictly archaeological sources.

CLIMATE   The climate and conditions of life have not changed very much. The spreading of population can be followed from finds and also place-names: the density increased in Western Europe as well as in Scandinavia, beginning already in the seventh century and reaching its height in the tenth. In Norway, for example, in the seventh century farms were being built on what is now exposed mountain heath: it is probable that the tree-line was slightly higher then, but human habitation was unable to maintain these outposts, and in the late Viking period finds from them cease, as they were deserted or became mere summer pastures. The lighter soils on sand and moraine were presumably already fully taken up: the heavier clays had to await the eighteenth-century draining to be usable as other than pasture.

We know very little at present of the houses, as the wood SETTLEMENTS of which they were built has not survived. But it seems likely that settlement included both isolated farms and village communities, probably in different proportions in different parts of Scandinavia. A farm at Edsviken, north of Stockholm, had one farm-house and a cluster of small sheds (including a smithy where iron was smelted and bronze cast). Where the farm road runs over the top of the ridge a runic inscription of the eleventh century is carved in the cliff: 'Atfari and Thorgils had the runes carved in memory of Horsi their father and Vidfari their brother.' On a little mound to the west of the farm is a burial-field. The dead had been burnt elsewhere, richly equipped, and their ashes were then brought here and covered with low mounds or stone squares and triangles. The farm has another cemetery too, beyond a marshy meadow, where the grave-mounds of very simple cremations are crowded. This was probably the slaves' burial-field.

Though farms like this were in intention self-sufficient, there were specialized craftsmen in the Viking period, vagabonds like the later scissors-grinders, and of one of them in Gotland we can have a very clear picture. His oak tool-chest (and two battered bronze kettles beside it) was found in 1936 by a farmer ploughing the bed of the dried-up Mästermyr lake. Perhaps it went overboard in summer, or through the ice in winter. Its owner was a versatile man: for heavy smithying he had heavy hammers, riveting block, nail-making tool; for lighter work files, and punches for ornamental work. He was a coppersmith too, with the special hammer for beating out copper kettles Plates 2, 3, 5 from inside, and a riveting cup, and shears with which the finder was still able to clip sheet metal. The craftsman pre-sumably used them to cut patches out of his battered vessels to repair others with. He was also a carpenter, with axes and adze, rasps, an excellent morticing saw and even a forerunner of the profile-plane for edging boat gunwhales and the like. One of his chisels is very reminiscent of a modern cooper's, and

Plate 4

he may have made barrels as well. The scales he used are care-fully marked and delicately ornamented, and suggest that he sold his work (such as the padlocks and the three large copper cow-bells) by weight. It is striking how similar his tools, from the late Viking period, are to those found right up to the begin-ning of the industrial period.

We find similar contact with the life of the age in the excava-tion outside Aalborg in Denmark, where part of a village and its grave-field has been cleared. It was crowded within a wooden palisade, and its burial field lay outside this on a mound over-looking the Limfjord on one side and the Kattegat on the other. The burials began on the top in the sixth century and then mainly continued down the southern slopes, like the annual rings on a tree. At the end of the tenth century the site was buried by a sand-drift as decisively as Pompeii by its lava, and has been undisturbed since then. When the sand was removed, the cemetery was revealed exactly as it was in the tenth century with the stones arranged in various figures, triangles, circles and squares; no vegetation had grown over them, and not a stone been moved. The ploughed fields ran

Plate 6

right up to the cemetery and one can still see the long narrow high-backed strips produced by ploughing towards the centre to make the land corrugated and self-draining; perhaps the sand came in the autumn after the ploughing. There was a road along the field, rather narrow, and one can see where a two-wheeled cart drove out over the furrows just before the storm.

When people built here again (this time on top of the old burial/field) fashions had changed. For the first time in Scandinavia we find here in the mid/eleventh century the farm built round an inner courtyard, which was to become the common South Scandinavian form. It gives shelter, and that was very necessary on the exposed side of the old burial/field above the Limfjord. Some of the buildings at Lindholm were supplied with solid timber fences, perhaps for the same reason.

A completely different type of site occurs only in Denmark— with a possible outlier in England at Warham Camp, near Wells in Norfolk. It consists of a circular military encampment surrounded by a large bank (which was originally palisaded) and a ditch. Inside the camp are carefully laid/out houses of which only the ground plans have survived. The houses are boat/shaped in plan and are set out in groups of four, round a central court/yard. At Trelleborg there were four of these groups, each set inside one quarter of the circular area. Trelle/borg on the west coast of Zealand, is the best known of these sites, having been published in 1948 by the excavator, Dr Poul Nørland. Recent excavations by Dr Schultz have un/covered a very important and much larger camp (with forty/eight houses) at Aggersborg, while the same excavator also investigated another similar camp at Fyrkat. A fourth camp exists in the centre of the present town of Odense and experi/mental investigations have been carried out to demonstrate its character.

MILITARY CAMPS

Plate 24

The extreme regularity of these camps indicates a discipline foreign to ordinary Viking civil settlement. It would seem that they were designed on a military basis but a theory that the population was exclusively masculine can be discounted by the fact that many female skeletons were found in the grave field at Trelleborg.

This camp is quite small when compared with Aggers/borg, using as the standard unit of measurement the Roman foot (11·613 ins.) the distance from the centre of the camp to the inner side of the circular bank is only about 234 Roman feet compared with 407 ft.; however, an extension became necessary at a later date and fifteen houses were built outside the wall and enclosed by another, lesser bank. It is perhaps in these great camps that we can see most clearly reflected the organized military nature of the late Viking period, when the Danes ruled over an empire which extended from the North Sea to the Isles of Scilly. If this is so the military forces com/manded by such kings as Canute and Svein must have been extremely powerful; it has been calculated by the excavator that the camp at Trelleborg would accommodate about twelve hundred men.

GRAVES

Plate 19

Such rare sites apart, we know the culture of the Viking Age best from its graves, often so richly furnished and of such variety. Many of the dead were cremated, but the mound was not always raised at the site of the burning. People thought that the dead, at any rate for a certain time, lived on in the mound, and thus supplied them with weapons, games, food and so on. But sometimes the burial is very simple, with the ashes col/lected into a clay pot and little by way of grave goods. We really know very little about their ideas of life after death. The eggs and small loaves in some of the graves are presumably con/nected with a belief in some sort of resurrection. One might cite a passage from a very detailed contemporary account, a com/ment the Arabic writer Ibn Fadlan received from a Viking in Russia, round about 920, explaining why they burnt their dead —'You Arabs are foolish to put those you love and honour into the ground, for earth and beasts and fields to eat them up: we burn them quickly, so they fly to Paradise in an instant.'

We have to remember that Ibn Fadlan was working through an interpreter: this reply cannot have been clearly understand/able to him and he may, as the word 'Paradise' suggests, have read more into it than was there.

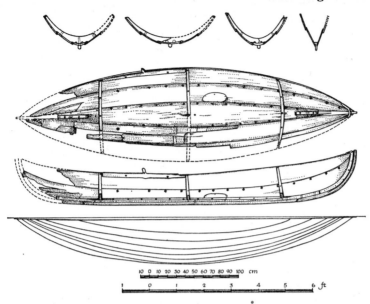

Fig. 1 The boat found in the Viking grave at Árby, Uppland

Occasionally one finds unburnt graves, both simple coffin graves and large chamber graves: they are frequent in Birka. As the orientation is often more or less east–west, it is possible that they show Christian influence. The most important un‑ burnt graves from the preceding period are the great boat graves along the water route at Vendel, Valsgärde, Tuna and Ultuna. For the whole of the Viking period (until they went over to churchyards in the late eleventh century) these important fami‑ lies followed the old fashion. But it is uncertain whether there is any connection between these boat graves, and the coffin and chamber graves. The latter were probably a continental importation by merchants and Ansgar's mission. They first became popular in southern Scandinavia and Birka, and are only sporadic elsewhere. For the whole of the Viking period cremation is the majority rite in mid‑Sweden, but in Skåne

33

inhumation is dominant and in Denmark the proportion of cremation to inhumation is about two to three.

Fig. 1

The unburnt boat grave was not the monopoly of the great yeoman families of Vendel, Valsgärde and Tuna. The Årby boat-burial north of Uppsala was unfortunately robbed in antiquity, but the procedure of burial can be clearly followed. The boat was lowered into a large hole, the dead man was laid

Plates 8, 9, 10 within it on a bed of grass and round him his weapons (later stolen) and domestic equipment. Then an Arab stallion was led down beside the boat and killed, as was an old greyhound. The boat was covered with planks, including old sledge-body side-rails, and then covered with earth.

There are eight similar small ships (twenty-footers) at Tuna in Västmanland, in each of which a woman is buried. In one an old lady lies on a bier, a straw mattress, wearing a splendid pearl necklace with silver pendant. The surviving pieces of ornamental weaves, oriental silks and multi-coloured borders hint at the richness of the clothing. In the bow were the utensils: bowls of wood and clay, frying-pan, dough-trough, storage jars, birch-bark box. By the bier were an elegantly turned beaker and a richly carved wooden spoon. The oars were ranged on the bulwark ready for the last journey. The men's boat-burials were evidently at a different site still undiscovered.

The best known of all the graves of the Viking Age are those in Vestfold in Norway—Oseberg, Gokstad, Tune, Borre, where the rulers of Vestfold lie in yachts like the Oseberg ship, or more seaworthy warships like those at Gokstad and Tune. The clay has there preserved the wood which elsewhere so often rotted, and for this reason they are the basis of our

Plate 7 understanding of the art and life of the period. The Ladby ship of about A.D. 900, from Fyn in Denmark, was also a long

THE GROWTH slender ship, well-suited to the work of a coastal guardship.

OF MARKET Though farms, villages and burial customs do not clearly

TOWNS divide the Viking Age from its predecessor, one cultural novelty does, and that is the professional merchant and the development of his home, the market town. This is first found in Scandinavia in the description of Gottfrid of Denmark's raid which we find in the Frankish annals under A.D. 804. He descended on Sliesthorp, on the border between Danes and Saxons, and four years later in his war against a Slavonic tribe, the Obotrites, destroyed their trading town of Reric (Rostock?) and shifted its merchants to Sliesthorp (Scandinavian Hedeby). The position of Hedeby, at the root of the Jutland peninsula, commanded the trade-route from the North Sea to the Baltic, and the town was a bone of contention between Danes and Germans: for a short time before Henry the Fowler's conquest of it in 934 it was also ruled by a mid-Swedish house.

Quite a lot of Hedeby has been preserved, most strikingly its huge semicircular earthwork surrounding the town, in places 30 feet high. This is not contemporary with the earliest levels of the town, and was often rebuilt. It encloses about 60 acres and is connected by a system of other earthworks with Hollingstedt, the port eleven miles away on the North Sea side of the peninsula. It stands on the banks of the Treene, which flows into the Eider up which ships from the North Sea sailed. Cargo from them was transferred to carts in Hollingstedt and taken behind the connecting earthworks to Hedeby where the Baltic ships awaited it. It was by this route that the gaily coloured cloths and luxury goods like spices and glassware came from Friesland to Scandinavia. Hedeby was a small town to begin with, and it was only in the course of the tenth century that it expanded to cover most of the ground inside the semicircle. A stream with piled sides ran through the town, with buildings along it ranging from 22 feet by 54 to 10 feet by 10, warehouses, dwelling-houses and small workshops. Each merchant's premises were enclosed by a fence of plaited hurdles. There was often a well in the enclosure, and those backing on to the river had steps down to the water.

Fig. 2

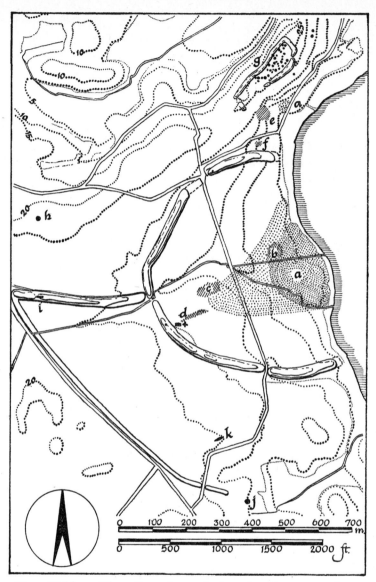

Fig. 2 Hedeby. a. The earlier settlement; b. the craftsmen's quarter; c-f. cemeteries of the Viking Period; g. the hill fort; h, j. earlier burial mounds; i. grave of the eighth century; k. boat grave

The first forcible transfer of merchants to Hedeby was followed, according to Rimbert's biography of Ansgar, by a flocking together of merchants from all parts to Hedeby. After a church had been built there, and the town had become safer for Christians, Rimbert tells us that Saxon merchants from Hamburg or Bremen, and merchants from Dorestad, freely visited Hedeby without fear, which before was not possible. The Saxons and Frisians were obviously of great importance, though whether any settled we do not know. A rather different view of the town in the late tenth century is given by an Arab, Ai-Tartushi, in his description of it as a large town, dirty and poor, its people living on fish and singing like the howling of dogs and worshipping Sirius. It may be that conditions in his day (the tenth century was less peaceful than the ninth) had worsened, but we must remember that his attitude to the inhabitants (who, he says, used an ointment which ensured that their beauty did not diminish with age) was that of a modern European tourist to primitive peoples abroad, a blend of romanticism and patronage. He is to be used as a historical source only with discretion.

Fig. 3

From Hedeby some goods went to Birka on the north-west side of the island of Björkön in Lake Mälar, the oldest known trading town in Sweden. We have two good descriptions of Birka, one in Rimbert's life of Ansgar about A.D. 870, the other about A.D. 1070 by Adam of Bremen (who had certainly never been in Scandinavia and derives from Ansgar). Modern scholarly interest in the place began with Hjalmar Stolpe, led to it by his interest in the amber found in the waters round Birka. He investigated its source, which proved to be the old trading town. He was told that he would find more by digging in the 'Black Earth' part of the island (which proved to be the site of the ancient town) than he would on the beach. Town, cemetery and fort have been intensively investigated since the eighteen-eighties, and as a result an extremely

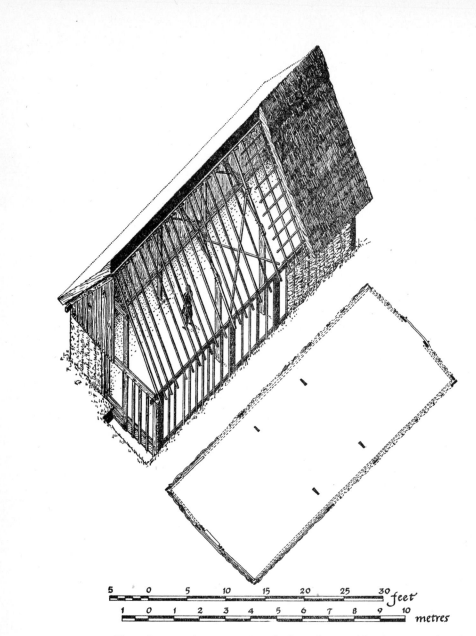

5   0   5   10   15   20   25   30 *feet*

1   0   1   2   3   4   5   6   7   8   9   10 *metres*

Fig 3 Axonometric reconstruction of a house from Hedeby showing wattle and daub construction

detailed picture of what may almost be called a Viking metro-
polis has emerged. The fort was built on the top of a 100-foot-
high cliff commanding the approach to the harbour. On the
western, cliff-protected side no wall was needed, but on the
other three a rampart of earth and stones 6 feet high and from
25 to 50 feet thick is pierced by only three gates. The northern
one looks across the sound to Adelsö Manor. It is now called
'The King's Gate' by the island's inhabitants, and it is quite
likely that Adelsö was a royal manor already in the ninth
century.

Plate 15

The town lies about 50 yards north-east of the fort with a
space evidently deliberately left empty in between. Though the
'Black Earth' belt got its local name from the fragments of
charcoal and organic material which make it much darker than
the island's other soil, there is no evidence that the town was
ever burnt. We have to deal merely with the domestic refuse of
generations. There were two types of house at least, one with
wattle-and-daub walls of intertwined twigs plastered with clay,
indicated by flat pieces of clay with the impression of the twigs
still visible. The other was the blockhouse constructed of large
vertical baulks of timber side by side. The gaps between the
baulks were caulked with clay and moss, and the long pieces
of clay, triangular in section, must have come from buildings
of this type. There is no reason to suppose that any difference of
time is shown by the two techniques. Other methods were used
atHedeby where it has been suggested they reflect a difference of
national tradition. In this view, the West German element
there used an inner planking wall, with an outer wattle-and-
daub one (cf. *wand*: 'wall'), and the Scandinavian one a wall
of vertical baulks. A similar mixture of populations (or of
traditions) would obviously not be out of place at Birka, but it
is quite impossible to draw any definite conclusion from these
two types of building. The town covered about 30 acres. It had
its own defences, of which only a 500-yard stretch running

Fig. 4

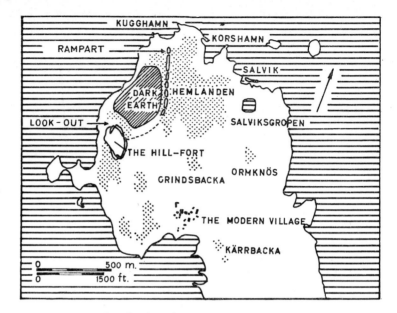

Fig. 4 Plan of Birka. The cemeteries are shown by the dotted areas

down to the Kugghamn (Frisian: 'cargo-boat harbour') in the
bay now survives. It presumably extended in the opposite
direction as far as the fort. The rampart, 6 feet high and
20–40 feet wide, runs along the top of a slight ridge, rather a
long way from the town. This was probably partly to guard
against the danger of incendiary attack by leaving a sort of
fire-gap between the town and the wall, partly because any
defences which did not include the ridge would have been
commanded from it. There are at the present day no less than
six openings in the rampart. As there can scarcely have been
need for six gates from the town to its cemetery, these are best
taken as the sites of vanished wooden towers. The earthwork
was probably surmounted by a wooden wall, like the well-
known ones surrounding later Russian towns.

The coast enclosed by the semicircle of fortification is mainly straight and open to the wind in three directions. The remains of heavy oak piling still visible are presumably the remains of jetties and breakwaters. One natural harbour, 'Krugghamn', has already been referred to: there was another, Korshamn, and farther to the east an artificially constructed basin with 180-foot sides, the Salviksgropen, which opens off a 200-yard-long lagoon with an artificial entrance. The large accumulation of ashes in a hollow facing seaward in the mound just west of the fort is probably to be explained as a beacon fire which would be visible far down the Södertälje Channel.

Birka was mainly a merchants' town, with markets both summer and winter. Graves in which the dead were buried with ice-crampons on their feet, and the large number of skates found, show that the freezing of the lake was not allowed to interrupt business. Winter is, after all, the best time for a fur market as the winter furs are the best, and furs, were among the main wares the merchants of Birka had to trade with their visitors for the silver and silk from the Orient, and the salt, clothes and household luxuries of Western Europe.

Plates 12, 14, 16, 17

Birka was thus very like Hedeby: like it originally unfortified, it was enclosed in the tenth century, an uneasy time in the Baltic. Indeed about A.D. 900 the site of the beacon fire was levelled, probably to close the gap the gently sloping hollow presented in the defences. The site yields an abundance of objects: weapons, pieces of mail-shirt, shield-bosses, knives, spear and arrow points, etc., but there were no feminine articles. It seems likely that the houses with beaten mud floors built up here held a garrison.

The third town in this commercial trio was Kaupang in Skiringsal on the west side of the Oslofjord in Norway. Here what may well have been the special cemetery of the merchants has been discovered in Dr Charlotte Blindheim's excavation. The graves are close together and uniform in style; the dead

Fig. 5

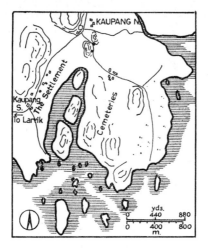

Fig. 5 Plan of Kaupang,
in Skiringsal

man is often buried in a boat, with his small elegant bronze balance (used to weigh the silver and gold used in payment) and stylish weapons and ornaments, often brought from England or Ireland. It may not be without significance that Ohthere after his voyage south to Skiringsal continued along the route to England, and that the name existed in such a thoroughly acclimatized native-looking Anglo-Saxon form as Scirincges Heal, for the archaeological material suggests a very strong connection with England.

Plate 18   Kaupang means 'the market-place' and the site differs from Birka and Hedeby significantly. It has an admirable natural harbour, and was protected on its landward side by high mountain ridges and the swamp between them. The excavations have shown that the buildings straggled between the ridge and the bay like a modern ribbon development. In the middle is an open field sloping gently to the bay, and it is tempting to suppose that this is the 'market place' and that there was no real year-round town. The absence of protective works would then be explained.

The sudden development of towns in Scandinavia round about A.D. 800 must be connected with a strengthening of royal power and a more stable social structure, even if it is at present impossible to relate this to what we know of the forma/ tion of the Scandinavian kingdoms. It has sometimes been supposed that Hedeby and Birka were Frisian trading colonies. There is no archaeological evidence that Birka was a Frisian settlement though it is certainly possible that there was at one time a Frisian trading station there. The reign of Charlemagne (768–814) and his organization of a State must be seen as the background for this development in Scandinavia.

The very excellence of Charlemagne's bureaucracy has per/ haps helped to distort our view of his State. Such detailed information is available to us about the organization of the royal villas, which were not simply self/sufficing agricultural units but also producers of manufactures 'for export' (mainly to the army), that they have bulked too large in our view of his State, leading historians like Pirenne to undervalue Charle/ magne's trading towns. In fact the royal villas accounted for only a small part of the country, but we know very little about the smaller free farms and villages, and to these must be added the towns and market/places, many of them founded in the early ninth century. It has been supposed that the towns did not play any important role, but this is difficult to reconcile with the fact that after 776 Charlemagne himself lived for about six months of the year not on his estates but in Aachen, Worms, Frankfurt, Würzburg, and Regensburg (when he was not campaigning).

Recent excavations at Wilhelmshafen and Emden have given a good idea of the Carolingian trading town founded about A.D. 800. They comprised wooden buildings along a single street at the end of which, in Emden, there was a little wooden church. Whilst the usual building of the area is a large one divided into two, for farm animals and people, these town buildings are smaller, with no provision for agriculture and are clearly merchants' houses by a good navigable waterway. Whether these towns were permanently inhabited, like Birka and Hedeby, or summer towns like Kaupang we do not know.

The two types of merchant we find in Scandinavia probably represent the open market and the town, respectively. They might be called the 'merchant-skipper' and the 'merchant-yeoman'. The first was a professional full-time merchant with no fixed place of business. As we meet him in later sagas he may arrive in Iceland in autumn, and, having laid up his ship, stay the winter with some farmer to depart again in the spring to the summer markets of Scandinavia. The second was not necessarily any less skilled as a seaman, but he was a man for whom trading voyages were only half his life. He had his own estate which he worked like any other yeoman farmer, and to which he normally returned each harvest time.

We can get a good idea of the life of such a man from the account of himself which Ohthere gave to 'his lord, King Alfred' some time in the 870's, which Alfred inserted in his translation of Orosius to provide a first-hand description of Scandinavia to supplement the rather remote one of this early fifth-century historian. That Alfred is called Ohthere's lord may give us a very important insight into his position to begin with. It may have been merely commercial diplomacy, like the custom described in *Egilssaga* whereby those Norsemen sailing to England usually had themselves given the *primsigning*, or first crossing, a sort of halfway baptism, 'so that they could have dealings with Christians as well as pagans, and continue to believe themselves as pleased them best.' Ohthere's furs would find a ready market in England, and his walrus ivory (of which he brought a sample to King Alfred) was a convincing (and cheaper) substitute for real ivory. The anglicized form of Norwegian words in Ohthere's account have given rise to various philological speculations, but they clearly imply a tradition of intercourse with Norway and are not mere nonce-words. When one thinks of all the English material in Kaupang it seems clear that a good connection at the English court was most desirable for a Scandinavian merchant. But Ohthere was perhaps a little more than this, for, though as yeoman he had 20 cows, 30 sheep, 20 pigs, and a little arable land which he ploughed with horses, his main wealth was in the tribute received by him from the Finns (Finnas). We have some reason to believe, from later Saga sources, that by the time of Ohthere's visit to Alfred this tribute had been seized as a royal monopoly by Harald Harfagri in his unification of the Nor-wegian kingdom, and was no longer the prerogative of such local leaders as Ohthere. It was the belief of Icelandic historians two centuries later that many of their forefathers had left Norway at this time because they were unwilling to accept Harald's overlordship, and Paasche suggested that Ohthere might have been a man who preferred to go to England instead. However this may be, the situation as Ohthere describes it to us, in which he 'living furthest North of all the Norwegians' collected tribute in furs, eiderdown, and seal and walrus-hide ropes from the hunting nomadic Finns of his region, was one which was passing away. He described to King Alfred a voyage of ex-ploration 'to see what lands there were' in commercial recon-naissance of whaling and walrus-hunting prospects. This took him round North Cape and into the White Sea where he found the whales disappointingly small, only 27 feet long com-pared to the 60-foot ones of his native region. The account of Ohthere which King Alfred gives us closes with a reference to another voyage, this time southward to Scirincges Heal and Hedeby (*aet Haepum*) which was reckoned to take over a month with favourable winds. It is followed by the account of another seafarer, Wulfstan, probably an Englishman, which carries the description of the route eastward into the Baltic as far as Truso.

That Ohthere (or Ottar, to call him by his own form of his name instead of the Old English one) visited Skiringsal and Hedeby does not necessarily imply that he traded there, though that seems most likely. The very existence of such towns was bound up with the long-distance trade of the professional mer-chant skippers, for they do not seem to have had any very close ties with their own immediate environs. The position of Hedeby shows quite clearly that it was essentially a town of transit trade, and indeed the finds from the area round it are markedly lacking in the imported wares in which it dealt. Some kinds of production could with advantage be carried on in such a town. Ornaments were cast in bronze and ex-ported over the whole of Scandinavia, and iron was smelted. Recent analyses of the slag shows that it was melted from Swedish iron ore, probably blooms from the marshes of Småland.

Birka was not so clearly as Hedeby exclusively concerned with long-range commerce. Its position was equally suited to become the centre of the internal trade of the rich surrounding area, and many of its imports from the Orient and Western Europe are in fact found in the rich graves of Uppland. Not all these, however, can confidently be attributed to the Birka trade, for there were other routes from the Baltic to the interior of mid-Sweden. But the long-range transit trade was evidently Birka's real concern, and when that decayed, so did the town. The position of Gotland in the trade of the Viking Age is problematic. In the eighth century there are signs of close con-nections with Western Europe, but these are completely lacking in the ninth century, so the trade route from Hedeby to Birka did not go via Gotland, but via Kalmarsund. However, silver hoards show that already in the ninth century oriental silver was reaching the island and in the tenth, connections with both east and west seem to have been close again. The as yet un-excavated site of Västergarn, south of Visby, may provide the answer. There, a semicircular wall reminiscent of those at Birka and Hedeby suggests that there may have been a trading town like them until it was covered by sand about A.D. 1000.

On the basis of the archaeological material one can, in spite of its limitations, make some attempt to answer the question of the relationship of towns to countryside. The expansion of population already mentioned continued into the Viking period, and finds from the period are more widely spread than from preceding ones. The area being exploited was widened, and whilst the increased production was in part taken by merchant-yeomen like Ottar, a good deal must have been handled by the professional merchant-skippers. How far was there a clash between these men of the trading towns and those like Ottar with roots in their own district of the countryside? We know of such a clash later, in Gotland in the thirteenth century, where the town of Visby in 1288 triumphed over its commercial opponents in the countryside. In the Viking period the reverse seems to have been the case. Birka and Skiringsal disappear and a generation passes before their place is taken; Hedeby was moved from its original site to a new one on the north side of the fjord. In Western Europe also, many important commercial towns disappeared at the same time; there is presumably some connection between these similar events, though it is not at present apparent. The first Scandinavian towns were a brilliant but short-lived contribution of the period when Scandinavia played a bigger role in world trade than it has since done until the present day.

The make-up of society in the Viking Age we learn from various literary sources. A very large number of free men lived on their own farms, where they had slaves for the harder work. As the production of the farm was generally low, it was usually combined with some subsidiary occupation such as hunting or fishing; it is not certain how far iron working was also carried on in this way, but it eventually became very important.

Districts that had previously been thinly populated, such as Småland, Gästrikland and Dalarna, but rich in marsh iron, became quite thickly settled on the basis of this iron-working, as the numerous slag heaps from this period show. And the graves are unusually well furnished with iron objects; sometimes the very grave-mound is made of slag. Such an increase of iron working cannot have been based on merely local needs, and we have striking evidence of the export trade in the shape

Plate 11   of a dozen axe-heads threaded on a stave found on the beach at Gjerrild Grenaa in North Jutland: they must have been part of the cargo of a wreck. The stave, with a knob at one end to stop them sliding off, was obviously designed for the transport of axe-heads in bulk. The other end was split and widened by a wedge to lock the heads on. The wood is spruce, which did not grow in Denmark during the Viking period, and analysis suggests that the iron is Swedish or Norwegian. The heads were not quite finished, as they had not been edged; that presumably was done just before they were sold. The find illustrates admirably the passage in the *Olafs saga helga* which tells of Canute sending from England to Kalf Arnarson in Norway for three dozen axes 'and let them be good ones'.

Most of the other trading wares have proved more perishable: furs, tar, wax, cloth and salt have left no traces. But the blunt-headed bone arrows used to shoot squirrel without damaging the fur, and the hairs from some Birka graves, show that squirrel, beaver and marten were traded. This demand for furs explains the wide distribution in the extreme north of material from the Viking Age, far up in the mountains of Lappland.

Plates 12, 42, 43   The changing silver hoards of southern Scandinavia reflect its changing, but always lively, contacts with the outside world. In the ninth century they are mainly of Arabic coins of the Eastern Caliphate and rings from Russia, with only a few Carolingian and English coins. In the early tenth century a flood of Arabic silver may represent not only increased trade but also the harrying of the Volga and the Caspian coast. About 960–970 the composition of the hoards changed. Byzantine coins appear, the Arabic coins are often of the Western Caliphate; elegantly granulated fragments of Polish work, and German coins from Cologne and Regensburg, reflect the increased importance of the trade route across Poland to Kiev, and from Wollin at the Oder's mouth. By A.D. 1000 the English (Danegeld) and German element dominates the Scandinavian hoards.

It was natural that this age of restless expansion and lively contact with other lands should live in the memories of subse-quent generations as a heroic age. On the other hand it has been often supposed by modern historians that it was forced upon a poverty-stricken people, compelled to expand by pressure of over-population in a land unable to support them all. As we have seen, whilst the archaeological finds certainly indicate a population which was increasing, they give no hint of poverty, but rather of increasing and firmly based prosperity. People have been struck by the fact that the Norwegians expanded to the mountains of Scotland, Iceland, Ireland (and in England particularly to the Lake District, Pennines and North York moors) whereas the Danes chose flatter countries, Friesland, eastern England and Normandy, and the Swedes the lakes and rivers of Ladoga, Ilmen, Neva and Volkhov, so like the Mälar area of Sweden. Of course one must not press this too far: one could equally find it quite natural that the route from Norway should be west, that from Denmark south, and that from Sweden east. But it may help to remind us that a considerable element of choice seems to have played a part in the direction of the Viking expansion, and this in its turn indicates the skill in navigation and confidence in their ships which were the natural resources exploited by the Viking raids.

CHAPTER II

British Isles and Atlantic Islands

IT IS NO GREAT DISTANCE across the North Sea from Scandinavia to Britain, and when the first Viking raids began, at the end of the eighth century, they were upon coasts already well known. Perhaps the political conditions were known too, for it is noticeable how, as in France and Russia so in England, a time of weakness and division contributed to the success of the Viking attack.

The early attacks (with the exception of the one recorded in the West Saxon Chronicle under A.D. 787, which has been doubted by some) were upon Northumbria, and in 793 'heathen men ravaged and laid waste God's church in Lindisfarne, robbing and slaying'. In the reaction to this first wave surprise is mixed almost equally with alarm. Alcuin says, 'We and our forefathers have lived here for about 350 years, and never have such terrors as these appeared in Britain, which we must now suffer from the pagans: it was not thought possible that such havoc could be made.' The attacks were interpreted as God's vengeance upon the people's unrighteousness, an inter‐pretation confirmed by the rain of blood from the roof of St Peter's, York, which had presaged them, and supported by Alcuin with a text from Jeremiah (1: 14): 'out of the north an evil shall break forth upon all the inhabitants of the land.'

The raid on Jarrow, the year after, was not so successful; a leader was killed, the attack repulsed, and some ships lost in bad weather. This may be why Viking activity was diverted in the next few years to the west coast and the Irish Sea.

It would be a mistake to conclude from the picture presented by the literary evidence that the Vikings crossed the North Sea to concentrate exclusively, or even mainly, on the plundering of Christian sites, and there is no evidence to convict them of specific animosity against Christianity (as distinct from more general avarice and brutality). The most important event of this stage of the Viking raids is not in fact mentioned by the chroniclers; they probably did not know of it and would not have included it if they had known. It is the settlement of the Atlantic Islands by the Vikings, which we learn from the archaeological material. The Irish monk Dicuil in his *De mensura orbis et terrae* of 825 speaks of some lonely islands in the Atlantic, uninhabited and nameless since the Creation, as having been inhabited a century earlier by Irish hermits ('sea-farers for the love of God' like the central figure of the Old English 'Seafarer' poem) who had in Dicuil's day abandoned the islands on the arrival of Scandinavian pirates. The written history of the islands after Dicuil's mention of them has been bedevilled by the erroneous views of the twelfth- and thirteenth-century saga writers in Iceland. They consistently tried to ex-plain the great expansion of the Viking Age as brought about by opponents of Harald Harfagri who preferred to leave Nor-way rather than submit to him after the battle of Hafrsfjord. This view was wrong, but it led them to modify the oral tradi-tional evidence available to them so as to agree with it. As they were also wrong by about thirty years about the date of the battle of Hafrsfjord, it will be seen that their evidence must be handled with the greatest care: often those parts of their narra-tives inconsistent with this scheme may be the most reliable parts of them.

The saga account of the Atlantic Islands is that Harald pur-sued his enemies to them, killed all the Vikings in Shetland, expelled them from Orkney and the Hebrides, found that they had all fled when he had reached the Isle of Man, and estab-lished the earldom of Orkney on his way home. It is extremely unlikely that any of this is true; archaeological material, place-names, and some references in Irish texts tell a different and more reliable story. The grave at Lamlash on Arran stands

THE
ATLANTIC
ISLANDS

alone from the eighth century, and its one-edged sword and early shield-boss are not exclusively Norse, but in the early ninth century Scandinavian graves become quite common in the Scottish Isles. This large scale colonization was connected with the activity in the Irish Sea about A.D. 800.

An Irish annal fragment from about 870 (i.e. before Hafrs-fjord) says that 'long ago', before the occupation of York in 866, a king's son Raghnall was expelled from Norway by his brothers and settled in Orkney. His sons from Orkney raided the Mediterranean (probably a reference to the 859 expedition described in chapter III). The name Raghnall is the same as the Rognvald the sagas connect with the earldom of the Orkneys, but it has escaped the tendency of the saga writers incorrectly to connect great figures like Rognvald with Harald Harfagri's time. The chronology of the account agrees with that of the grave-finds in suggesting that the islands were settled at least two generations before Hafrsfjord (*c.* 900). Torf-Einar, Raghnall's son (and successor as earl) is said to have got his nickname from the introduction of peat as fuel on the treeless islands, and his descendants ruled them for the next three hundred years. *Orkneyinga saga* gives a vivid picture of the stormy times, full of blood feuds and revenges. The great days of the Orkney earldom were under Sigurd Digri (who fell at the battle of Clontarf in 1014) and his son Torfinn. Sigurd's rule extended southwards under his magic Raven banner, as far as Fife.

The situation in Shetland is more obscure. There the law code was the ordinary Norwegian *Gulatingslag*, whereas Orkney seems to have had its own laws: the church was later directly under Norway, and this suggests that the Scandinavian inhabi-tants of Shetland were more closely connected with Norway, and had less independence than those of Orkney.

The Hebrides seem to have belonged to a different world, looking towards Ireland and Iceland rather than the homeland

Fig. 6 Reconstruction of the Jarlshof settlement. Late eleventh century

of Norway. This impression may be partly due to many of the founders of great Icelandic families having come to Iceland via the Hebrides, as a result of which the sagas naturally preserve more detail about the connections of the Hebrides with Iceland. According to *Eyrbyggja Saga* the first Norse chief in the Hebrides (it must have been some time before the middle of the ninth century) was Ketill Flatnose from Sogn. His daughter, Aud the Deep-minded (one of the earliest Christians in Iceland) married Olaf the White who was king of the Norse colony in Dublin from 850 to 871. Later sagas like *Laxdæla* as usual advance the date of all this to Harald Harfagri's day.

The Norse settlement at the beginning of the century was confined to the islands, though there were odd attacks on the mainland. In 839, sixty-five Viking ships raided Dublin and then left for Scotland, where King Eoganam and others were

Plate 27

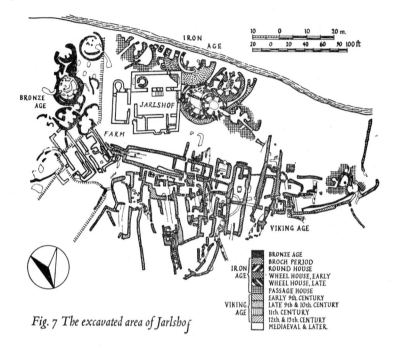

Fig. 7 The excavated area of Jarlshof

BRONZE AGE
BROCH PERIOD
ROUND HOUSE
WHEEL HOUSE, EARLY
WHEEL HOUSE, LATE
PASSAGE HOUSE
EARLY 9th.CENTURY
LATE 9th & 10th.CENTURY
11th.CENTURY
12th. & 13th.CENTURY
MEDIAEVAL & LATER.

IRON AGE

VIKING AGE

slain. At the end of the century, after the Norse kingdom of Dublin had been established, ships based on Ireland raided Scotland in 892, 900 and 904. More than half the Scandinavian graves on the islands belong to the ninth century, but all the fifteen from the Scottish mainland with one exception belong to the tenth. It is perhaps not a mere coincidence that Jarlshof in Shetland is a Viking manor established in the ninth century, Freswick in Caithness in the late tenth. Settlement in the Islands preceded by some generations that in Scotland.

Fig. 6

Jarlshof (the name is an invention of Sir Walter Scott, not an Old Norse inheritance) is the classic site for the understand‚ ing of life among the Vikings on the Atlantic Islands. It was excavated by Dr A. O. Curle 1931–35, Professor Gordon Childe 1937–39 and Mr J. R. C. Hamilton 1949–51. It lies on a small point on the west side of the natural harbour of Sumburgh Voe formed by the gentle northern slope of the land from the 200-foot cliffs of the island's southern edge, and seems to have been first occupied at the end of the Stone Age about 2000 B.C. Some descendants of the earlier inhabitants, and their wheel- and their passage-houses, were probably there when the Vikings arrived in A.D. 800–850 after a 200-mile voyage. The newcomers built near the ruins their typical two-roomed rectangular dwelling-house, the walls of stone with an earth core, turf and stone alternating on the north side (as in Iceland) to hold the warmth better. The living-room was about 40 feet long, with benches down each wall and a long fire down the middle of the room. The kitchen, which had an oven built into one wall, was 16 feet long.

Fig. 7

One outhouse, 12 feet by 13, with a hearth is more likely to have been a bath-house than a temple, and another with a hearth was perhaps the native serfs' dwelling.

A smithy and a byre complete the estate. The kitchen refuse (from ox, sheep, pig, red deer, whale, seal, fishes, and many birds) gives a good idea of the housekeeping. Domestic animals were the terrier and the pony (the latter somewhat bigger than the present Shetland pony). The usual finds of boat-rivets, knives, arrowheads are represented, and combs and bone needles having shapes and ornament well-known from Norway. Of more interest, though no great works of art, are the small figure drawings on stone tablets which are quite unusual, and perhaps depict two of the first generation of settlers. One depicts a young bearded man with curly hair and round staring eyes wearing a high-collared tunic. On the other side is another bearded man, but older, perhaps toothless.

Fig. 8

Some generation after this first building the farm was ex-panded: a new dwelling-house, the same size as the first (which was enlarged), was built at an angle to it and the outbuildings were improved, so that the settlement took on somewhat the air

Fig. 8 Engraving of a man's head on a stone tablet, Jarlshof

of a village. It seems to have been a peaceful, rather parochial existence (very few foreign objects are found) not what one would have expected perhaps in a half-way house between Norway and Scotland in a tumultuous Viking Age.

THE ISLE OF MAN   Written references for the early history of the Isle of Man are scanty. There is nothing between the first raid of 798 and the (Danish) one of 853. After this the island's connections seem to have been with the Vikings from Ireland. In 973 Magnus Haraldsson, King of the Islands, was one of the kings who accepted Edgar at Chester. The scantiness of written reference is more than compensated for by a wealth of other material, runic crosses and Viking graves. The island's central position between Ireland, Scotland, England and Wales meant that it responded to many different influences as political conditions changed: it is the only one of the Viking colonies which has preserved continuously unbroken traditional elements of its original constitution like the lawman and the Thing (that of Iceland is a twentieth-century revival).

Most of the grave-finds are of tenth-century date, but it seems most likely that the Viking kingdom on Man took shape in the second half of the ninth, at the same time as those in Dublin and York, with both of which it had such lively artistic and political connections. The graves in Man resemble very closely contemporary ones in western Norway. The mound from about A.D. 900 at Knoc y Doonee excavated by P. M. C. Kermode was large even by Scandinavian standards, 50 feet in diameter and 8 feet high. Inside was a 20-foot boat of 8-foot beam (no narrow ship one notices), of which decayed wood and iron rivets remain. Its owner was buried with full equip-ment; sword, spear, axe, shield, his horse properly bridled, and the craftsman's tools (in this case hammer, knife and black-smith's tongs) so characteristic of Norwegian graves. Another boat grave contains a silver belt ornament of Continental work-manship of the second half of the ninth century. These are not uncommon in Scandinavian graves, and its presence on Man suggests that perhaps Vikings from there had taken part in some of the ninth-century raids on the Carolingian kingdom. Other less splendid graves are more interesting in another way. About half a dozen swords come from as many graves in the churchyards of Jurby, Kirk Michael, St Maughold and else-where. Such graves with weapons are also known from church-yards in Scotland and England but are there less common. The Vikings in the West seem to have gone over easily to Christianity, and their society must have contained every degree between paganism and Christianity: the owners of some well furnished, apparently pagan, graves probably called them-selves Christians, whilst the presence of the sword in a church-yard grave (and some of the motifs on the crosses themselves) suggest how qualified was the Christianity they represent. It is presumably this 'mixed' belief that is responsible for the com-parative rarity of the unambiguously pagan rite of burning in the British Isles. Only half a dozen such Viking burials are

known, two from Orkney and one each from Arran, Cumberland, Derbyshire and Dublin.

Most of the Viking runic inscriptions of the period in the
British Isles come from the Manx crosses, which have twenty-
nine. Ireland has three and Scotland and the other islands another
twenty (excluding the much later Maeshowe ones). The early
Manx crosses are purely Celtic wheel-headed ones: the Viking
settlers did not take over this pattern, but borrowed a Celtic
type from Scotland (whence they had presumably come), a
flat rectangular slab with a wheel-headed cross incised upon it.
The oldest group is best represented by one at Kirk Michael,
erected by 'Melbrigdi son of Aðakan the Smith, but Gaut
made it and all in Man'. Evidently the man who adopted the
pattern and introduced it to Man, between 930 and 950, was
called Gaut. His work and that of his successors has been
studied in detail by P. M. C. Kermode and Haakon Shetelig.
In Gaut's day Man had been a Viking colony for a century,
but we see that two of the names in the inscription quoted are
Irish. Forty-four names occur on the crosses, twenty-two Norse
and eleven Irish, and the language also suggests a mixed population. The changing blend from 930–1000 of Celtic and Scandinavian elements in the ornament tells the same story. Gaut
has interlaced bands and a simple key pattern of Celtic origin,
and split bands and a ring chain perhaps of his devising. It is
found in Cumberland and North Yorkshire, and Kermode
thought Gaut must have learnt it there in his youth: it is
equally possible that the influence was the other way. Gaut's
younger successors introduced a pictorial element absent from
his own work; they showed, as well as simple animal portraits
of Scottish type, Sigurd Fafnisbane, Odin's fight with the
Fenriswolf, the Doom of the Gods and so on. The really significant development, however, is the arrival of the Jellinge-
style animal ornament. This originated probably in Scandinavian Yorkshire, but it is the further developed form from

Scandinavia which is reflected in the Isle of Man, suggesting that the island's direct communications with Norway were as good as its very good communications with York.

After the diversion of their attentions to the West and the Islands referred to above, it was not until 835 that a real attack was made upon England (the Isle of Sheppey) by the Vikings. In 844 and again in 860 and 861 the same fleet attacked both sides of the Channel, just as those in the West had raided both Ireland and Scotland. Though Vikings had wintered in Thanet as early as 851, it was not until 865 that the first attempt at conquest as distinct from plunder was made. One force arrived in Thanet and concluded an agreement with the men of Kent. The Great Army which came to East Anglia, accord-ing to Scandinavian tradition, was seeking revenge for Ragnar Loðbrók, and was led by his sons. Their names, Halfdan, Invar, Ubbe, occur in the Anglo-Saxon Chronicle account, by far the best contemporary description in any land of a Viking invasion. The detail of the campaigning of the next ten years is best followed in its dispassionate account. From it one can see the greatest advantage of the Vikings, their high mobility, which was reduced by Alfred's careful, largely organizational steps to obstruct them by building camps and blocking rivers or to compel them to use up their mobility uselessly by inter-posing his army between them and their objectives. After ten years of this, in 875, the Chronicle shows that one of the three brothers, Healfdene, divided out the lands of the Northum-brians among the army, and they began to plough them. A part of them thus ceased to exist as traditional Viking raiders. In 880 the Danes went into East Anglia, settled there, and shared out the land. Their movements from 865 to 883, which the Chronicle describes by the formula, 'In this year the great army went . . .', were as follows: first to York to profit from internal dissension there, and then to Mercia, but in '69 back to York. Into East Anglia again, defeated in the attack on

ENGLAND

Fig. 9

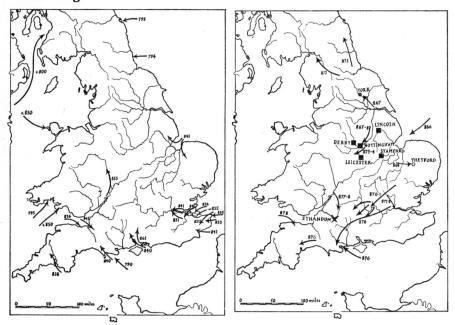

Fig. 9 The Viking attacks on the British Isles. I. During the first half of the ninth century

Wessex in '70, to London in '71, Torksey on the Trent in '72, westwards to Repton in '73, in '74 some back to Northumbria and some to Cambridge, to continue harrying southern England, until their departure to raid the Continent in 883.

Famine on the Continent drove them back, with new additions like the famous Hasteinn, to begin the second great campaign in 892 by landing from two hundred and fifty ships (this time carrying their own horses, which had previously been procured after they had landed) and overwhelming one of Alfred's half-built forts manned only by a few of the local inhabitants. But the campaign was a more decided English victory than the first. For four years the Viking army was now held up by its numbers of wounded (and enduring the daily attacks of patrol from Alfred's army seeking battle), now

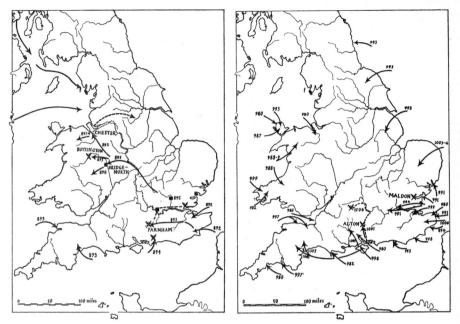

II. Later ninth century until 878. III. The years 892 until 895. IV. During the tenth century

moving fruitlessly into the wilder west of Britain, shepherded by Alfred's army behind it, between it and its sea routes. In 896 the members of this army too followed Halfdan's example, some in East Anglia and some in Northumbria. The Chronicle says of 896, 'And afterwards in the summer of this year the Danish Army divided, one part going into East Anglia and one into Northumbria; and those that were moneyless got themselves ships and went south across the sea to the Seine. By the grace of God the army had not on the whole afflicted the English people very greatly; but they were much more seriously afflicted in those three years (the plague) by the mor⟋tality of cattle and men.'

This was the beginning of Scandinavian England, with communities like the Five Boroughs (Lincoln, Stamford,

Leicester, Derby and Nottingham, all originally strategic Roman towns) and the kingdom of York, and it differed from the unambiguous conquests in Ireland, Scotland and the Islands. The Danelaw lands lay north-east of the Thames–Lea–Bedford–Ouse–Watling Street line, and remind us of Scandinavia by the large percentage of freemen listed in the later survey of Doomsday Book, and the prominence of the town.

The place names are also often Scandinavian: they are not always good evidence of the state of affairs in the great days of the Danelaw, however, as many may be the product of the Scandinavianized dialect of the medieval peasantry of northern and eastern England, so that their testimonial to the strength of the Scandinavian settlement is a rather indirect one. And the indirect Anglicization of the Danelaw, in spite of such agreements about separate law and custom as that between Alfred and Guthrum, must have begun the moment it was set up.

There was a strong Scandinavian influence on its English inhabitants in return. It must be remembered that extreme nationalism is a late historical phenomenon. England had been previously divided in small kingdoms, internal strife was no novelty and the Danes could be readily accepted. Edgar's decree of 962 illustrates this very well. 'It is my will that there should be in force among the Danes such good law as they best decide on, and I have ever allowed them this and will allow it as long as my life lasts, because of your loyalty which you have always shown me.' This loyalty had been manifested under the most trying circumstances. Already in 907 it had been necessary to repair the Roman fortifications of Chester as a protection against Norwegian raiders from the Irish Sea, and the recovery of the Danelaw is presented in English sources, such as the poem on the retaking of the Five Boroughs, rather as a fight against its new Norwegian (and heathen) overlords than its original Danish (now often Christian) inhabitants.

Daene wæran ær
Under Norðmannum nyde gebegde
On hæþenra hæfte clommum
Lange þrage oþ hie alysde eft
. . . Eadmund cyning.

'The Danes were before this subjected to the Norwegians by force, for a long time captive in bonds to the heathen, until King Edmund redeemed them.' After 918 all England south of the Humber was ruled by the English king, and the kingdom of York was the only remaining independent Viking colony. Rognvald from Dublin, King in York, submitted in 920, and his successor Sigtrygg Gale was baptized (which may be the reason his compatriots gave him his nickname 'crazy') and married Æthelstan's sister. On his death in 926, Æthelstan took over York. Sigtrygg's brother Gudrod resisted: he was captured by Æthelstan and very well treated, but could not bear to remain at Æthelstan's court, for as a later chronicler tells us, 'he was an old pirate, accustomed to living in the water like a fish'. Two years before Æthelstan's death in 939, Olaf Kvaran recaptured York, and after Æthelstan's death the situation in York was constantly changing, though one of its brief kings seems to have called himself 'rex totius Britanniae' on his coinage. Olaf Kvaran had two reigns, as did the notorious Eric Blood-axe after his expulsion (for excessive cruelty) from Norway. His killing on Stainmoor (probably in flight from York) in 954 marks the end of the Viking kingdom of York. Just as much as the rest of the Danelaw it had been an Anglo-Scandinavian civilization, and it was in fact much more productive than the rest in those areas of culture which depended on uniting two different traditions—new styles in sculpture, new metres in poetry, very good coinage with traditional motifs, perhaps even a written chronicle to Scandinavian tastes. But the tone of the society was different, and more violent. We are given a masterly depiction of the relationships involved in

Egilssaga, but one incident from the Anglo-Saxon Chronicle may be quoted as symbolic. In 943 Olaf, still heathen, raided the Midlands, and was trapped by Edmund in Leicester. Trapped with him was Wulfstan, the Archbishop of York. The Vikings of York retained their mobility and traditional manner of life and this was their cultural importance: for as they retained close links and good communications with the Celtic lands and Scandinavia, the elements which they avidly absorbed from Anglo-Saxon civilization were brought into fertilizing contact with other widely differing ones. The result was assured of wide circulation, so that a process begun in York (like the evolution of Jellinge-style animal ornament) might be developed further in Norway or Denmark and then be returned again, perhaps via Dublin or Man.

This is quite different from the situation in the more settled southern Danelaw. The excellent coinage of York is typical.

Plate 35   At this date no other Scandinavian kings coined their own money, but the York kings, taking over this English medium, were the first kings to use the vernacular word (as distinct from Latin *rex*) on their coins. R. H. M. Dolley's studies have shown the size and importance of this coinage, made by English mint-masters like Edelferd for kings like Gudrod; almost every surviving example of his 'raven' coin, for instance, is from a different die: probably desire for royal prestige combined with real need to produce such a large currency so quickly. It is striking that Olaf Kvaran's son Sigtrygg Silkybeard was the first king in Ireland to coin money. David Wilson has suggested that the Arabic *dirhems* found together with these Viking coins in hoards from eastern England to Ireland, must have come from Scandinavia, and in payment in the course of trade.

England was free from further trouble with Vikings until 980, when fleets raided Southampton, Thanet and Cheshire. In 991, Olaf Tryggvasson (later King of Norway) raided with ninety-three ships. Byrhtnoth died heroically at Maldon in the battle celebrated in the last heroic Old English poem, giving the Danes 'spear points instead of silver for tribute', and Dane- geld was paid for the first time, to the tune of £10,000. The sum rose steadily: £16,000 (994), £24,000 (1002), £36,000 (1007), £48,000 (1012). In 1013 with King Svein's arrival in the Humber, it was again a matter of conquest rather than raiding. He was naturally accepted by the Danelaw: he died in 1014, but his son Canute remained in England and on Ethel- red's death in 1016 was chosen king over the whole of England. In 1018 England paid £72,000 (and £10,500 from London) to groups of the Army leaving England. As in the earlier struggles between English kings and Vikings not all the latter were on one side, and it is to this period that Freeman's famous phrase 'The monarchy of Cerdic was now confined to the decks of 45 Scandinavian warships' refers. Æthelred in 1013 took refuge on the ships of Thorkell Havi, a former plunderer of England who had martyred Archbishop Ælfheah, but now a convert (of a kind) to Christianity and Æthelred's most reliable supporter.

Canute ruled in relative peace until his death in 1035. Whilst it was presumably the influence of his court which led to the recrudescence of Scandinavian taste in southern England (shown by such magnificent carvings as the Guildhall tomb- stone), it was evidently his aim to be an English king, and he Plates 31, 32 no doubt wished to be remembered as he is depicted in the well-known Winchester drawing: as a patron of the Church in traditional style (with only the pommel of the characteristic Viking sword visible beneath his cloak). It is in some ways more difficult to form an idea of the relationship between Danes and English in this period than in earlier ones. The special nature of the population of the Danelaw (no doubt becoming steadily more Anglicized) seems to have been accepted in general, though in 1002 'the king [Æthelred] ordered all the Danish men who were in England to be slain on St Brice's

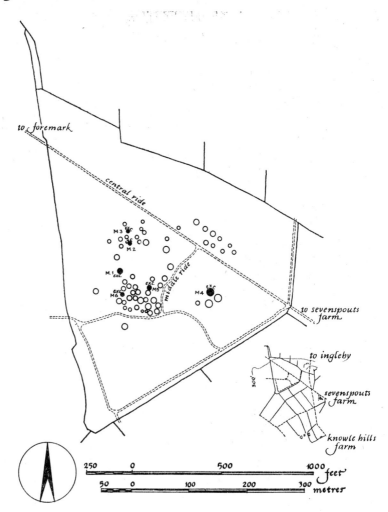

Fig. 10 Plan of the cemetery at Ingleby, Derbyshire. The filled-in circles mark the excavated graves up to 1954. Nine more have been excavated since then

day [13th November] because the king had been told that they wished to deprive him of his life by treachery, and all his coun, cillors after him, and then seize his kingdom.' How far this massacre was carried out we do not know. Nor is the less sensational evidence for the blending together of the two cul, tures much more definite. Someone about A.D. 1000 writes, 'I tell thee also, brother Edward, now that thou hast asked me that you [i.e. the English nation] do wrong in abandoning the English practices which your fathers followed, and in loving the practices of heathen men who begrudge you life, and in so doing show by such evil habits that you despise your race and your ancestors, since in insult to them you dress in Danish fashion with bared necks and with your hair over your eyes.'

Apart from the evidence of period and place names and institutions, archaeological evidence of the nature and extent of the Scandinavian population of the British Isles is rare. Not only the influence of Christianity in England, but also the rarity in Denmark of large burial mounds like those of Norway and Sweden explain this. Graves which were poorly furnished in a heathen milieu at home would not be better equipped in an English churchyard, and finds like the battle,axe from Repton churchyard are exceptional stages of the mixture of heathen and Christian, which can also be seen on the crosses from Middle, [Plates 29, 30] ton which depict heathen burials complete with axe, sword, spear, shield, and perhaps even the sacrificed cock IbnFadlan refers to. The most impressive Viking cemetery in England is that at Ingleby, Derbyshire, where there are 60 mounds, vary, [Fig. 10] ing from 20 to 45 feet in diameter, and from 18 to 60 inches high. Some of them cover quite richly,furnished cremation burials. Elsewhere Viking graves are scattered, only two being known from the Five Boroughs and two from Yorkshire, rather more from Cumberland and Northumberland. There is one boat,burial from Walthamstow and perhaps another from Pembroke, with a further twenty from the islands. The

majority of the objects from the Viking Age are chance finds
Figs. 11, 12, 13 from river-beds (whence many Viking swords have been
Plate 28 dredged) and from town sites such as London and York.
IRELAND The Vikings first came to Ireland in a raid on Lambay
(north of Dublin) in 795. Ireland, having escaped the Roman
administration of the rest of Western Europe, had preserved the
Celtic clan-society, a mass of small kingdoms which at the
Fig. 14 beginning of the ninth century when the Vikings appeared
were grouped under the two over-kings of south-west and
north-east, the latter the famous kings of Tara.

*Fig. 11 Viking spear-head inlaid with silver and bronze, from the River Thames.
Length 46 cm.*

The Church introduced in the fifth century by St Patrick
also differed from that of the Continent in its strong hermit
tradition and the development of quasi-university schools from
the original scattered cells of one or two hermits. It was the
wealth of these monasteries which attracted the raiders. The
Annals of Ulster say in 820: 'The Ocean poured torrents of
foreigners over Erin, so that not a harbour or landing, fort or
stronghold, was without fleets of Scandinavians and pirates.'
In 836 two fleets, each of 60 ships, came up the Boyne and the
Liffey and harried all Meath. In the same year the first Viking
colony in Dublin was established, and in 841 it was fortified
along with other sites on the Narrow Water by Carlingford, at
Linn Duachail in Louth, and at Linn Roio.

Turgeis (Thorgils) the first of the sea-kings arrived in 839,
'king of all the strangers in Erin' until his capture and execution
by drowning in 845. There can scarcely have been a formal
Norse kingdom in his day, though he may have exacted a sort
of Danegeld. He called himself abbot of Armagh, and his wife

chanted heathen spells on the cathedral's high altar. The chronicle accuses him of attempting to convert the whole island to the worship of Thor, but this is very unlikely. His death was followed by a rising against the Vikings, the standard figure for whose losses in a defeat in the Irish chronicles is 12,000. The figure is given for the defeat of Haakon in 847, that of Tomkrair (Thorgeirr?), and of the heathen of Derry (leader unnamed). Whilst the exaggeration of the chronicles is evident, it was clearly a bad time for the Vikings and had it not been for the disunity of the Irish, Ireland might have been rid of them. In

Fig. 12 Viking sword, from the River Witham at Lincoln. Length 107 cm.

850 the Black Strangers (Danish Vikings) arrived, and harried Dublin. Next year they seized the Norse camp of Carlingford. According to the chronicles, the battle at Carlingford between Danes and Norwegians killed five thousand Norwegians of good family; the triumphant Danes, honouring a promise given to the Irish high-king's messengers on the battlefield, surrendered a large chest of gold and silver to St Patrick, 'for the Danes had at least a kind of piety; they were for piety's sake capable of ceasing for a while from their eating and drinking.'

The different Vikings were united in 853 under Amlaibh (Olafr Huiti). He is said to have come (like Turgeis) 'with a royal fleet', and with instructions from his father the Norwegian king about what taxes to demand. There may indeed have been some deliberate reinforcement from the homeland to meet an obviously dangerous situation. Olaf left Dublin to return to Norway after an 18-year reign and was succeeded by his brother Ivor. The occupation was thus on a formal colonial basis: Irish kings maintained their positions, some co/operating with the ruling power (and intermarrying), others opposing it. From the former arose the *gall/gaidil* or 'foreign Irish', Irishmen who had deserted their faith and were the foster/sons of Vikings whose way of life they adopted. Their leader, Caitill/Finn (Ketill Hviti) was a Norwegian.

In 865–870 Olaf made three expeditions to Scotland, and after Ivar's death in 874 Olaf is called by the *Annals of Ulster* 'rex Nordmannorum Totius Hiberniae et Britanniae'. This per/ haps indicates that Norwegians had already established a foot/ hold in north/western England. The following year Halfdan

Fig. 13 Comb-case from Lincoln (the comb is reconstructed). Length 14 cm.

from Northumbria led a force against Ireland 'because Ivar had invaded Northumbria'. The next half/century was to be full of coming and going between the two Viking kingdoms of Dublin and York. Sigtrygg, Ivar's son, invaded England in 892 but returned to Ireland in 894, and was murdered in the following year by one of his own band. Again the death of the leader led to a native rising. In 901 the Irish recaptured Dublin, the Vikings fled to the Isle of Man and Scotland, and for twelve years Ireland enjoyed comparative peace under Cearbhall.

The Vikings returning in 913 in a four/year campaign recovered the whole of Ireland, and their grip was not shaken until 980. Their two great kings in this period were Gudrod (rex Crudelissimus Normannorum) until 934, and the cele/ brated Olaf Kvaran (who may indeed be the original Havelok the Dane). He was from the Northumbrian kingdom, son of the Sigtrygg Gali who became its ruler in 921, and he fought at

Fig. 14 Ireland, showing the principal sites of the Viking Period

ULSTER

Bangor

Armagh•

•Sligo

Carlingford•

CONNACHT

LEINSTER

Lambay

Howth•

Dublin Clontarf

Clonmacnoise

Arklow

•Limerick

MUNSTER

Wexford

Waterford

10 0 10 20 30 40 50   100 miles

Brunanburh in 937. From '41 to '44, and again from '49 to '52, he ruled in York as well. He married a daughter of the king of Leinster, and was related through a cousin with Maelsechlainn, king of Meath. It was his involvement in the feud between these two that led to his fall. In 980 he was

defeated at Tara, and his son Ragnvald fell: three days later
Dublin was in flames. Olaf withdrew to the monastery of Iona,
became a monk, and died a year later. His fall did not free
Ireland from the Vikings, and nine years later Olaf's son,
Sigtrygg Silkybeard became king in Dublin, and took part
(on the side opposed to the one that his father had favoured)
in the old feud between Meath and Leinster. He was defeated
by Brian Boru king of Munster in A.D. 1000 and Ireland was
united for the first time under an Irish king by Brian in 1002.
Brian was a good administrator, and under his reign there was
peace for ten years (a long time in Ireland). He was an earnest
supporter of cultural advance, and devoted a third of his
revenues from Wales and Scotland to the endowment of arts
and scholarship. His heavy taxes (particularly on cattle) made
Leinster revolt against him. The dispute provided opportunity
for troops from Scotland, Wales, Flanders and Normandy, and
for Sigurd Digri who came from Orkney. In the great Irish
victory at Clontarf on Good Friday 1014 Brian fell together
with his brother, son and grandson, and so did Sigurd. But
Sigtrygg Silkybeard had followed the battle from the protection
of Dublin; he reigned another twenty years, to go on Christian
pilgrimage and raid on his return. It would be wrong to see
Clontarf as a nationalist rising of Ireland against the invaders.
The battle became so celebrated in story because of the great
men, Brian and Sigurd, who fell. A verse on it is included in
Njals saga:

> I was there when warriors fought
> Swordblades rang on Ireland's coast
> Metal yelled as shield it sought
> Spear points in the well-armed host.
> I heard sword blows many more
> Sigurd fell in battle's blast
> From his wounds there sprang hot gore
> Brian fell, but won at last.

The written sources are full only of battles, exaggerated armies, and taxes. Nothing is said of Dublin as a Norse centre in Ireland. There is no hint of any colonization such as took place elsewhere, in England or the Atlantic Islands. The absence of Scandinavian place names confirms this. The specialized nature of relatively small garrison forces in Dublin and other places, and the fact that they were early converted to Christianity explains the rarity of Viking graves in Ireland. Only one large cemetery is known, from the site of Kilmain-ham Hospital in Dublin. From it come about 40 swords, most of the ninth century and some richly ornamented. There are 35 spears and 30 shield-bosses, but only six women's graves, all from the ninth century and one from the beginning of it. It appears that the women had accompanied the settlement at its foundation.

Elsewhere in Ireland finds are very scattered, and there are only three runic inscriptions, all showing a mixture of Irish and Norse elements. One is on part of a sword-belt from Green-mount, 'Dufnall Seal's head owns this sword', and another on a part of a stone cross in the cathedral at Killaloe, 'Thorgrim erected this cross', with a further inscription in the Celtic ogam alphabet, 'Beandac(h)t (ar) Toreagr(im)'—'a blessing on Thorgrim'. The third with the inscription: 'Lir erected this stone; M . . . carved (the) runes', is found on a stone which was first set up as a monument and some time later used as a lintel in a house on the island called Beginish, Co. Kerry. They date from the eleventh century and show how Irish and Norse had blended together by that time. Archaeological material con-firms the often rather dubious written sources in the view that the Norse held Ireland mainly as a fortress-base for other opera-tions and did not attempt to colonize it; hence the accounts of their extortions from the population. Had there been a Norse population these would probably not have been so frequent.

73

CHAPTER III

The Continent

THE EARLIEST CONNECTIONS between Scandinavia and the Continent seem to have been of a peaceful kind, based on trade. It is true that one hears of one or two isolated raids by Scandinavian seafarers, but they are exceptional. This commercial contact increased steadily, and was strengthened by the missionaries who came in the steps of the merchants. It is about the year 700 that we hear of the first missionary to Denmark, Willibrord, the Apostle of the Frisians, who left Utrecht for the North. If his mission did not have much effect, it at any rate demonstrated the Church's awakening awareness of and interest in Scandinavia.

THE
FRANKISH
EMPIRE

At the very beginning of the ninth century the Empire of Charlemagne had been greatly expanded northwards. The Saxons had been overcome, and the Elbe was the Empire's border. Denmark was in dangerous proximity to it, and it must have seemed quite likely that Charlemagne would not halt his expansion on the Elbe. Gottfrid is the first Danish king to emerge as a real person from the ranks of the apparently mythical saga-heroes who preceded him; so little is known of him, and of the nature of his control of his kingdom, that it would be dangerous to attribute to him a foreign policy in the modern sense. One has the strong impression, however, of a consciously defensive policy behind such enterprises as the raid on the Obodrites and their trading town of Reric. The whole of the Frisian coast had at this time been subjected to Charlemagne, and the Frisians were the traditional traders of Northern Europe. Gottfrid did not content himself with the booty from the sack of Reric, but forcibly transplanted its merchants to his own new trading town of Sliesthorp and immediately fortified its communications and his southern frontier with Charlemagne's dominions. The Frankish annals describe his measures: 'He ordered the kingdom's frontier against the Saxons to be fortified with a rampart so that the rampart from the eastern arm of the sea which the Danes call the Baltic [lit. East Salt-water] to the Western Ocean could protect the whole north bank of the Ejder; it was to have only one gate, through which wagons and riders could pass in and out. After having apportioned the work among his generals he returned home.' The respect which appears in this Frankish account should be set off against the irony with which Einhard, the biographer of Charlemagne, refers much later (after 830) to Gottfrid. 'He regarded Friesland and the Saxons completely as his own possessions, and will no doubt soon come to Aachen with a strong army.' The irony was somewhat mis-placed. Gottfrid's first reactions to the Carolingian expansion appears not to have been exclusively defensive, as his attack on Reric shows, and his arrangements at the frontier were intended to prevent his large neighbour from securing a tight grip on the trade of Scandinavia through command of Friesland.

In 810 Gottfrid invaded Frisia with a fleet of 200 ships, defeated in three separate engagements the organized coastal defence to which Charlemagne had devoted such attention, and demanded 100 pounds of silver in tribute.

When Charlemagne died in 814 he left to his son and suc-cessor Louis the Pious an Empire protected, when danger threatened, by fleets in its rivers and levies from the whole coastal population. One of Louis' most important measures was the maintenance of his father's organization. He was suc- *Fig. 15* cessful in this, and between 814 and 833 attacks on the Frankish coast by Vikings are mentioned only in 820. In this year thir-teen ships attacked the coast of Flanders, but were put to flight with some casualties. In the same year ships came to the Seine, but the pirates lost five men and were driven away. That two such occurrences should have been thought worth

Fig. 15. Map showing the Viking trade routes

WALRUS
IVORY
ROPES
FURS

FISH
WOOL
TALLOW

WALRUS
FALCONS
FISH

TIMBER

FURS

FURS

Kaupang

Birka

LEATHER
WOOL
JEWELLERY

Limerick

Dublin

York

Hollingsted

Grobin

AMBER

Waterford

London

TIN
WOOL
WHEAT
HONEY

Hamburg

Wollin

Truso

Hedeby

Dorestad

Quentowic

Rouen

SALT

CLOTH GLASS
WEAPONS
JEWELLERY

Noirmoutier

WINE

Byzan

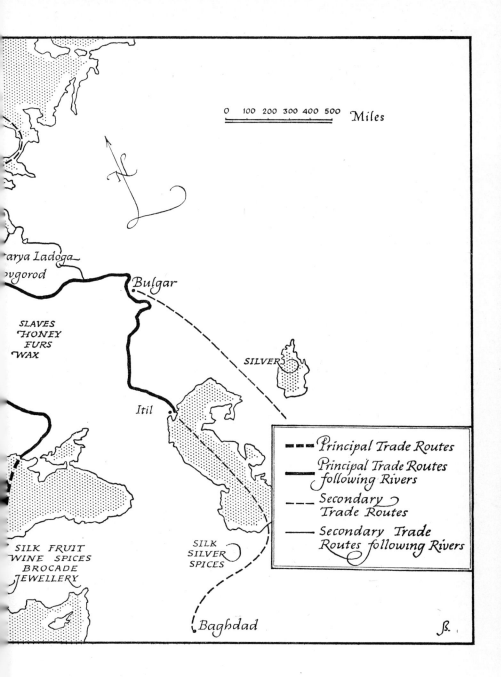

0   100 200 300 400 500 Miles

arya Ladoga
vgorod

Bulgar

SLAVES
HONEY
FURS
WAX

SILVER

Itil

SILK FRUIT
WINE SPICES
BROCADE
JEWELLERY

SILK
SILVER
SPICES

- - - *Principal Trade Routes*

―― *Principal Trade Routes following Rivers*

- - *Secondary Trade Routes*

―― *Secondary Trade Routes following Rivers*

Baghdad

ß.

mentioning in the annals suggests that there were no real raids whatever on the Empire's territory in this period. But the Vikings were above all professionals in their attitude to piracy, and after this demonstration that Louis had maintained the coast defence there were no further attacks until, as a result of inner dissensions, it had again become sufficiently weakened. In 834 the immensely wealthy but undefended trading city of Dorestad was abandoned to a Danish raiding fleet which made straight for it after some merely perfunctory sacking of the coast. This must have assured the Vikings that no resistance was to be met with, and it marked the beginning of the serious Viking inroads upon the Frankish Empire, though not until after Louis' death in 840 do we hear of large organized campaigns. Whilst his sons fought one another for the empire, the first Danish fleet under Asgeirr entered the Seine and burnt Rouen, pillaging up river as far as St Denis, and next year Quentowic, a principal port of the English trade, was sacked. The three great trading towns of the Empire, Dorestad, Rouen, and Quentowic had all been plundered. In 843 Nantes, crowded with celebrants of John the Baptist's feast, was attacked; on the island of Noirmoutier, abandoned by the monks because of earlier attacks, the raiders established themselves, 'as if they meant to stay for ever' said the annals. This is the first reference to an established winter base: the Vikings concerned were *Westfaldingi* from the west side of Oslo fjord, but they had probably come to the Loire from the Viking kingdom in Ireland. Noirmoutier had a lively trade with ships coming from all parts of Europe for salt and the wines of the Loire, and the Viking flag followed the trade.

After the death of Louis, Lothar, the oldest son and future emperor, was left with a narrow strip of territory running across the middle of Europe from Italy to Friesland, pressed in between the wider territories of his brothers Charles the Bald in the west and Ludvig in the east. In his unequal struggle against them he had great employment for Scandinavian mercenaries, and indeed it seems that in some decisive engagements both sides were, as it were, represented by professional teams of Vikings. In the disturbed conditions of those times it is, how ever, likely that it was always more profitable to engage in private plundering enterprises than to act simply as the agent of one of Louis' sons, and most of the Vikings who flocked to the Empire probably did so on their own account. It was prob ably for this reason that Lothar gave the island of Walcheren in Friesland to two brothers Harald and Rorik to secure their allegiance against other Vikings and against his own brothers. This was the first step on the road which led to Rollo receiving Normandy in 911. The Harald concerned may have been the fugitive claimant to the Danish throne who was baptized at Ingelheim in 826, and rewarded for his conversion with Rüstringen at the mouth of the Weser. Certainly the leaders of such ventures were often not simply private venturers. The fleet of six hundred vessels which burnt Hamburg (and almost killed St Ansgar) in 845 had been sent by Horek, king of Denmark, and the fleet of one hundred and twenty ships which sailed up the Seine in the same year was led by a Ragnar who was probably the celebrated Ragnar Loðbrók. The coastal defences were no longer effective. Paris fell to them, and Ermentarius of Noirmoutier writing in the 860's gives a vivid impression of the unhappy times:

> The number of ships grows: the endless stream of Vikings never ceases to increase. Everywhere the Christians are victims of massacres, burn ings, plunderings: the Vikings conquer all in their path, and no one resists them: they seize Bordeaux, Périgueux, Limoges, Angoulème and Toulouse. Angers, Tours and Orléans are annihilated and an innumerable fleet sails up the Seine and the evil grows in the whole region. Rouen is laid waste, plundered and burnt: Paris, Beauvais and Meaux taken, Melun's strong fortress levelled to the ground, Chartres occupied, Evreux and Bayeux plundered, and every town besieged.

Scarcely a town, scarcely a monastery is spared: all the people fly, and few are those who dare to say, 'Stay and fight, for our land, children, homes!' In their trance, preoccupied with rivalry, they ransom for tribute what they ought to defend with the sword, and allow the kingdom of the Christians to perish.

Ermentarius very likely exaggerates, and clearly has his eye upon the great men who were more concerned with their revenues than defence. Sometimes a spirited resistance was offered, as in the siege of Paris in 886, and Abbon's versified description of it may stand as a counterpart to Ermentarius.

The town trembles, and horns resound, the walls are bathed in floods of tears, the whole region laments: from the river are heard the horn blasts. Stones and spears one on top of another fly through the air. Our men give a loud battle cry which is answered by the Danes. Suddenly the earth shakes (as a tower falls): our men lament, the Danes rejoice. Reinforcements fighting bravely try to reach those groaning in the tower, but in vain.

More and more often attacks seem to have been bought off. Danegeld is well known from England: it is often overlooked that we first meet it in France, whence the Vikings probably took the idea to England. Their raids in France, unlike the first settlements in England, seem to have been comparatively brief affairs designed to extract it. Charles the Bald in 845 appears to have been unwilling to pay, but was induced to do so by his nobles who disliked the idea of a strong central monarchy, and were able to ensure that the burden of the Danegeld lay upon the peasantry and not upon their own estates. The 7,000 pounds of silver paid in 845 secured peace for seven years, but in 852 (on the ninth of October) two new leaders, Sydroc and Gottfrid exacted Danegeld from the Seine area. The next payment was in 860, but was of a very curious kind. A group under Bjorn had established a Viking base on an island in the Seine, called Oscellus, probably near Jeufosse, and in 856 and 857 plundered Paris. The king's efforts to get rid of them were hampered by a revolt of his nobles, to suppress which he had to raise a twelve-weeks' siege of the island.

In 859 a new Viking fleet under Weland arrived in the Somme and began to plunder. There was an obvious clash of interests between the two Viking raiders, and in 860 Weland offered to annihilate the island Vikings for 3,000 pounds of silver. The king accepted and set about raising the money by a tax on farms, churches and on all merchants, even the poorest; this was a sort of *heerbann*, originally a payment for exemption from military service, and the surplus remained in the exchequer, so that the collection of Danegeld was profitable for others besides the Danes. Complete inventories were required to calculate it. The process took so long that the price was raised to 5,000 pounds of silver, and much corn and cattle as well. A contemporary saint's life tells us that the sum was paid in gold as well as silver: gold was not used as coinage at this time, but some fine gold work probably from a Reims workshop of the early ninth century has been found at Hon in Norway, and it is not unlikely that it was part of a Danegeld. Having collected payment from Charles, Weland's Vikings duly overcame Bjorn's men on the island and took in booty from them a further six thousand pounds of silver. This exploitation of the Frankish kingdom continued until 926. Thirteen Danegelds were levied and the total of the seven whose figures are known is 39,700 pounds of silver; in 866 food and wine are included, and it is specifically provided that the silver shall be weighed according to Scandinavian measures; indemnity is to be paid if a Scandinavian is killed; further, the Vikings are to keep the slaves captured, and if one escapes he is either to be returned or paid for. The previous informal robbery has given place to large-scale organization.

The Viking inroads reached their peak from 879 to 892, to which time belongs the well-known '*A furore Normannorum libera nos'* prayer. The respite in 892 was caused by a famine which diverted the raiders to England until 896.

The annals in France have a gap from 900 until 919: it is in this period that it became a Norse dependency of the Frankish Throne. It seems that Rollo and his men had from their arrival in 900 been seeking land rather than plunder, and in 911 Charles the Simple, unable to prevent their advance, gave Rollo Normandy perhaps on certain conditions like his other barons. Rollo put it on a sound footing and when Robert, Count of Paris, led a revolt against the king and triumphed, the Normans continued to resist his forces. The new king, Rudolf, was eventually compelled to come to terms with them and pay in 926 a Danegeld of a slightly different kind. This was the last occasion on which Danegeld was paid. When Normandy came under a Norse administration, new bands of Scandinavians arrived and from the place-names and the names of the agricultural terms it seems that at least part of the farmers came from the Danelaw in England.

It seems possible that the *taille* of later French feudalism, a tax levied at the lord's discretion on his subjects, derives from the arrangements for collecting Danegeld, but the Vikings left few material traces on the mainland of Europe. There is a grave at Antum near Groningen in Holland from which two swords, two spears, a shield and a stirrup are Scandinavian, of the late ninth century. Another is at Pitres, between Rouen and Paris, and is shown by the two oval bronze brooches to be a woman's grave of the same period. The most striking and most challenging of the three Viking graves is certainly that on Ile de Groix, off Lorient on the south coast of Brittany. There a mound on top of a cliff was being slowly eaten away by the sea when in 1906 it was investigated by du Chatellier. The mound, 5 yards high and about 20 in diameter, covered a burnt area 6 yards by 5 yards and 6 inches thick, over the whole of which were found 800 rivets and 200 nails and fragments of 15 shield-

Plates 36, 38

Plate 37

Fig. 16

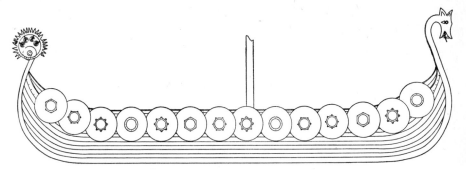

Fig. 16. Reconstruction of the Ile de Groix ship

bosses. In the centre was a large iron cauldron, surrounded by weapons and smith's tools. One of the swords was well pre-served; some of the spears had been deliberately bent before being deposited. There were ornaments such as small silver buckles and clasps for holding up stockings, and a gold finger-ring and small beads of melted silver; some gold and silver wire from a rich cloth also survived. Dice and playing pieces, saddle accoutrements and drinking-horn mounts are also recog-nizable among many unidentifiable fragments.

It is clear that we have here a ship-burial of Viking type (the ship was built of oak, but its mast and oars were pine, which did not grow in that part of Brittany). The Viking rite of burning in a boat, though common in Norway and mid-Sweden, is rare in the Viking settlements in the West. Not enough survives of the ship, which was probably a forty-footer, for us to learn anything of its structure, but in one detail it supplies a gap in our knowledge of the Viking ships—a cir-cular band 2 feet in diameter with movable leaflike ornaments round the outside and three rings inside. It can have had no practical purpose, and was evidently meant to be seen from both sides: it was not nailed on to anything else, for there are no holes. It seems most likely that this was the 'dragon's tail', mentioned in sagas, which balanced the figure-head at the bow. This we know was often a dragon, not only from the name 'dragon-ship' but from provisos in the oldest Icelandic laws to prevent these terrible gaping heads from frightening away guardian spirits. One of the Gotland carved stones (from Smiss in Stenkyrka) shows a very similar stern ornament.

The rite of burning in a ship is a Scandinavian one, and one of the swords too is Scandinavian, though the other might have been made anywhere. One spear is of West European origin, the others are Scandinavian in shape, but the shield-bosses and most of the other material are quite un-Scandinavian. The absence of anything specifically Irish tells against the view that the dead man came from Ireland, and the amount of foreign material makes it clear he had not come direct from Scandinavia. He was probably one of the Loire Vikings, or from Normandy, and is our only representative of the mixed culture of the Vikings on the Continent to compare with the mixtures in Ireland and in the Danelaw. Ile de Groix is isolated in the Atlantic, and lying as it did on one of the great maritime trade-routes of Western Europe, must have made an excellent den for pirates. The man burnt there together with a younger person (perhaps a woman) in his ship was perhaps a Scandinavian sea-king. He may well have lived abroad for a long time, perhaps been a second-generation Scandinavian from Normandy or from the Loire region.

About five hundred earthworks of different shapes and sizes are known from Normandy. Very few have been excavated and studied, so that they can not as yet be dated or fitted into any context. We know from the annals that the Vikings did build earthworks, and presumably some of those in Normandy are of their construction.

Hague-Dike, an earthwork running across the peninsula of La Hague, west of Cherbourg, is a completely Scandinavian name (*haga*: enclosed area, *dike*: bank) in an area rich in

Scandinavian place-names. It cuts off the last five miles of the peninsula between two deep bays, including the only good natural harbour between Normandy and the Loire, and was built to defend a population living out on the point from attacks from the landward side. It is thus tempting to assume that it was of Viking construction like Trelleborg and the Danavirke. As the result of joint excavation by the universities of Caen and Lund in 1951–52 its structure was shown to resemble closely that of earthworks of known Scandinavian workmanship; but when the carbon 14 method was applied to the charcoal from the ramparts' structure it yielded a rather surprising result. The earthwork dates from the Hallstatt period, 800–900 B.C. This does not exclude of course the possibility of its re-use during the Viking period, and the place-names show that Vikings certainly settled there, but it does mean that it cannot be compared with Trelleborg and the Danavirke as a Viking fortification.

The Vikings' inroads upon the Continent were not con- fined to the North Sea and Atlantic coasts. One of the most splendid kingdoms of Europe (and an important intermediary between the East and Europe) was that of the Moors in Spain. Its wealth was famous and must have presented a temptation to many a Viking contemplating an expedition. Very few con- temporary Arabic sources have survived, so that we are depen- dent on later recensions which often seem to quote the lost sources verbatim. These later writers use the name *al-Majus* (fire-worshipper, wizard, heathen) for the Vikings, just as, though from a different religious view, the Anglo-Saxons referred to them as 'the heathen'. But it is not certain, though it is certainly possible, that *al-Majus* from the beginning had this meaning. A thirteenth-century Arabic writer Ibn al-Atir, whose work derives from the tenth-century al-Tabaris, tells us that Alphonso II in his resistance to the Moors in 795 was helped by *al-Majus*. When we remember that Alcuin in 799 writes of 'the heathen' harrying the coast of Aquitaine,¯there seems no reason to doubt that the Vikings had reached Spain as early as the end of the eighth century. The first raid of which we can be certain was in 844, when the walls of Seville were destroyed. According to Ibn al⁄Quītīyah (died 977) the Vikings went on to North Africa and Italy, and even reached Alexan⁄dria, but this feat properly belongs to the expedition of 859, under Hasteinn and Björn.

It is of this expedition that Dudo of St Quentin tells his entertaining story of the sack of 'Rome'. Flushed by success in France, the Vikings could be contented with no lesser booty than that of the world's greatest city, and set off to besiege it. The defences of their objective proved too strong and they had to resort to cunning in order to gain entrance; they pretended that their leader had died and that they desired for him Christian burial. Once the bier was safely inside the town the 'dead' Hasteinn leapt from it and ran the bishop through. After this supposed triumph the news that the town was not Rome, but the little seaport town of Luna drove him to a frenzy.

How much truth there is in the story of this expedition is doubtful. A Viking expedition did leave the Loire in 859 and return in 862 but was probably led by men from Ireland, who would know the old sea⁄route from Ireland to Spain. It is presumably not coincidence when we hear of black slaves being sold in Ireland soon after this expedition.

In Spain, the opposition to the Vikings seems to have been a good deal more resolute (as well as more scientific) than it was in France. This is shown by the account Ibn al⁄Quītīyah gives of escaping Vikings protecting themselves against attack by threatening not to ransom the prisoners they had on board, and then ransoming them for clothes and food, not gold and silver. The science appears in the equipment of the fleet built by the Emir of Seville. The marines (recruited from Andalusia) were furnished with good weapons and naphtha, presumably for incendiary use in something corresponding to a modern flamethrower. Against a tarred vessel built of resinous soft/ woods and depending for its mobility on rowers who would in those latitudes be stripped to the waist this must have been a most effective weapon. It may be significant that the sixty/two ships of the famous expedition of Björn and Hasteinn in 859 soon left Spain after harrying Algeciras, and raided more ex/ tensively on the African coast before choosing France for their winter quarters, where they would want to be undisturbed. They settled in La Camargue in the Rhône delta. From their fortified base in La Camargue they raided up the river as far north as Nîmes, Arles and Valence. They were eventually defeated, whereupon they sailed along the Italian coast, raiding Pisa and probably continuing into the Eastern Mediterranean. Their return through the Straits of Gibraltar in 861 was op/ posed by the Saracen fleet, and of the original sixty/two Viking ships only twenty/two returned to the Loire from which they had set out. As the ransom at Pamplona of the Prince of Navarre alone amounted to 90,000 denarii they probably still considered the expedition to have been profitable.

The interval between this and the next Viking raid on the Spanish peninsula, almost a century, is nevertheless a convin/ cing testimonial to the effectiveness of the Moorish resistance. There were fleeting visits in the interim, but even the next organized raid, in 966, was comparatively small, comprising only twenty/eight ships. It was defeated. In 970, rumours are recorded in Moorish Spain of the imminent arrival of another Viking fleet—'May Allah curse them'—but nothing came of them. The rumours were not entirely unfounded, for the Christian kingdom of Asturias in northern Spain did in those years suffer from Viking attacks, eighteen cities, including Santiago de Compostella falling into Viking hands. Some part of the fleet concerned was presumably sighted by the Moorish defences.

The Mediterranean and Spain, it is clear, lay at the extreme fringes of the Vikings' sphere of activity. But this of course did not stand in the way of some peaceful connections with the Moors; the initiative in these probably lay with the Moors, but the report of the despatch of ambassadors to Viking kings by the Emir of Seville may not be correct. The trade route must have run along the Atlantic coast to Ireland. A number of the Arabic coins found in Viking Age hoards in Norway were

Fig. 17 Imitations of Arabic script on a pair of leaden weights from a grave at Kiloran Bay, Colonsay

minted in Moorish Spain and North Africa, and they pre, sumably arrived in Norway via Ireland. When the Irish in 968 seized Limerick from the Norsemen, the booty is said to have consisted among other things of ornate foreign saddles and magnificent variegated silk garments, scarlet as well as green. These certainly sound like Moorish imports. The grave of a Viking merchant on the Hebridean isle of Colonsay marks this trade route a stage further north. It is from the late ninth cen, *Fig. 17* tury, and contains a pair of leaden weights which are decorated with enamelled bronze plates the ornament of which is clearly derivative from Arabic script. This imitation is in its way a more telling indication of a widespread taste for Arabic im, ports than the presence of even genuine Arabic script could have been. This trade route of the west is, however, less docu, mented than the other source of Near East material, the trade of the Swedish Vikings in Russia, and has not been so inten, sively studied.

CHAPTER IV

Swedish Vikings in the East

THE SWEDISH EXPEDITIONS eastward were very different from those of the Norwegians and Danes in the West
—those sailed over the open sea against organized though dis-
united kingdoms. The wealth of the countries was concen-
trated, a convenient target for plunder. In the East the Swedes
had to follow the rivers through huge tracts inhabited only by
Finnish and Slavonic tribes before they reached the frontiers of
the Arabic and Byzantine states. The wealth available was
natural resources of furs and slaves which were to be traded
with the Orient. Later the Swedes succeeded in taxing the
native population, and in the tenth century there were some
purely plundering ventures of the type familiar in the West.

The most important literary source for this activity is the
early twelfth-century Nestorian Chronicle, a history of the Scandinavian princes of Kiev. Its material is drawn from Greek
annalists, perhaps some older diarists, and two or three peace
treaties between the Greeks and the Scandinavians. The more
imaginative portions are probably based upon warriors' reminiscences, a Varangian saga formed in South Russia; some of
them were included in Icelandic sagas, for it was a memorable
thing in the life of any Northern warrior that he had formed part
of the Varangian Guard, the Scandinavian mercenaries of the
Eastern Empire. The Nestorian Chronicle tells of the expulsion
of the Scandinavians after their first attempts at taxation. Because of the subsequent disorder they were called back again,
and three brothers, Rurik, Sineus and Truvor, returned. After
his brothers' death Rurik settled in Novgorod and took over
the whole kingdom. This is not a reliable account of the begin-
nings of the Swedish eastward expansion (it is reminiscent of
Widukind's story of the Saxons) which was mainly in the

Volga region, where the Nestorian Chronicle (like the early Anglo-Saxon Chronicle) was concerned only with the immediate origins of its own royal house.

More certain evidence comes from the Frankish *Annales Bertiniani* which tell us that in 839 Louis the Pious received in Ingelheim an embassy from the Byzantine Emperor Theophilus. It was accompanied by some people of Swedish race calling themselves Rhos (the first time we meet the term). They had been sent by their prince to Constantinople to negotiate, but were unable because of savage tribes to return the way they had come. Theophilus asked that they might make their way home through Louis's dominions. The name Rhos later became the standard name for the Scandinavians in Kiev, and the name Russia is derived from it. Its etymology has given rise to many theories, the most probable that it represents *rodr*, 'the rowing road' which gave the Finnish name for Sweden, Ruotsi. Rus was used only of Swedes in Russia, not in their homeland. The Scandinavians with the embassy said that their king was called the '*chaganus*', the same title as was used by the Khazars north of the Caspian and the Bulgars of the middle Volga: they probably came themselves from the upper Volga. The title *chacanus* is also used by the Arabic author Ibn Rustah writing of the Rus in the early tenth century.

THE LADOGA
DISTRICT
It has thus been supposed that by 839 there was already on the upper Volga an independent Swedish State organized after the local model of the Bulgars or Khazars, but this is only hypothesis. Archaeological evidence shows that Swedes were at this time in contact with the Orient along the Volga route. The *kolbjäger* of the sources were probably Scandinavian fur-traders organized in some sort of guild: the word is evidently taken from Old Norse *kylfingr*, a club member, and reminds one in this of *felagi* (English 'fellow') which was similarly used, as in a runic inscription at Hedeby, of shares in a venture. Their commercial activities made necessary fixed stations for the col-

lection and exchange of their wares, but only one of these of the ninth century has so far been excavated, at Staraja Ladoga (Old Norse: Aldeigjuborg). It is sited not (as were Birka, Hedeby and Wollin) by the sea, open to surprise attack, but eight miles up the river Volkhov at the mouth of the Ladoga river, and an earth rampart encloses an area a little under quarter of a mile square. The site is on the high river bank by a ravine   Plates 40, 41 which gives further protection, and the earth has preserved the remains of the wooden buildings. Excavation began there in the eighteenth century, but it is only with the excavations of Rav-donikas since the Second World War that it has been possible to form a clear idea of the site.

The literary sources of information about Aldeigjuborg found in various Old Norse sagas are all late and unverifiable. The oldest concerns an event supposed to have happened at the end of the tenth century, when Earl Erik is said to have burnt the town. It appears from the archaeological evidence that the town had then been in existence for a long time, though exactly how long cannot be determined. The levels of the ninth and tenth centuries on the site contain much Swedish material but it may well be that there was already a town of some sort there when the first Swedes arrived. Nor can we know whether they seized it by force, or gained permission to use it by negotiation. From the ninth-century layer comes a bow with a runic inscription which though difficult to decipher is perhaps an extract from a heroic poem:

> Above, the frost-giant eagle-cloaked,
> The plaguer of the shining moon,
> And mighty plougher of old.

Poems in descriptive praise of weapons (though in their case on shields) are attributed to the two earliest skalds, Bragi and Thjodolf, and there is nothing strange in a poem in praise of an

ornamented weapon at this early date which is about contemporary with them. Its discovery may even help to strengthen
the case for the existence of such complicated skaldic poetry as
early as this; Bragi was considered the founder of the highly
professional complexities of skaldic poetry, and appears in the
kennings, or riddling metaphors, of later skalds as a semi-divine
patron of poetry; and Thjodolf is scarcely more than semi-
mythical as far as our knowledge of him goes. It is striking that
this poem from Staraja Ladoga, however interpreted (the
version given above is based upon Gerd Höst's), is certainly as
obscurely allusive as the much later fully-developed skaldic
verse of the tenth century. The frost-giant is Tresvelgr who lived
at the end of the world in the extreme North, the moon's
plaguer (or spoiler) is the giant Skoll or Skati who in Norse
mythology ground up the sun and moon to eat them, and the
plougher is Gefion (a deity mentioned by Bragi in one of his
poems) whose oxen ploughed away the Danish island of
Sjelland.

There is evidence of continuous habitation in Staraja Ladoga,
and the site was not merely a fortress refuge, but a fortified town.
The houses were crammed together and when one fell into
ruins another was quickly built on top of it. Repnikov's view
was that the early layers (before the ninth-century Swedish
material) suggested an originally Finnish community, but
Ravdonikas on the (scarcely conclusive) evidence of the simple
pottery believes the original inhabitants to have been Slavonic.
The type of building used by the inhabitants of Staraja Ladoga
was at first a large double-roomed one, succeeded in later layers
by small square one-roomed cottages with an oven in one
corner, like the later Russian peasant cottage. Ravdonikas has
suggested that this shows a change in the social milieu of the
inhabitants, an earlier collective organization being succeeded
by a family one early in the tenth century. But one might also
argue that the large timber hall, unusual in Slavonic lands,

represents the original Finnish or Scandinavian settlers and the later cottages a Slavonic immigration or the influence of local usages.

The question of the affiliations of the first inhabitants of the town will only be solved when its burial ground is found. This has not yet been done, though there are many mounds along the rivers Volkhov, Sias, Voronega, Pascha and Ojat covering a large area south and south-west of Ladoga and also along the Svir, the main route to the East, between Lakes Ladoga and Onega. About four hundred have been investigated (some not very satisfactorily) and two types have been distinguished. One of these types is believed to be Finnish, whilst the other con-tained Swedish objects. The first Swedish settlers arrived in this area in the mid-ninth century, up the Neva and across Lake Ladoga. Some remained, whilst others pushed on the long road to the Volga, across Onega, southward down the Vytegra until it turned east, when the boats had to be dragged overland to the Kovscha, and thence sailed via Sjenksa to the Volga, already half a mile wide where they joined it. Thence the journey was easier to the great trading town of Bulgar in the Volga bend.

In the late ninth and tenth century the Ladoga district was in part gradually colonized by Swedish settlers, on good terms with the native population, probably Finnish, which they found already settled there. Only in that event could they have safely expanded as they did in the tenth century, probably from Staraja Ladoga, to the whole area south-east of Lake Ladoga. A consequence of such relations was that the Swedish immi-grants gradually became assimilated to the local Finnish popula-tion and also the arriving Slavonic population. They appear, however, to have preserved their characteristic customs, clothes, and weapons for at least another century, and perhaps longer.

The reason for so great an expansion of Swedish colonization in this district cannot be certainly determined. The great importance of Staraja Ladoga was partly because it lay where one of the great Scandinavian roads to the East divided into two, the Volga route and the Dnieper route. To a certain extent it controlled trade on the river Volkhov, but it was perhaps not a very important trading town itself except as a transit town, where merchants might rest on their arduous journey. On the other hand, the extended colonization in the area away from the town can scarcely have had anything to do with trade but was more probably an affair of land-hungry emigrants.

SOUTH RUSSIA AND THE CASPIAN There could be no such Swedish settlements on the Volga, where large towns had been long established on the fur-trade route. Ibn Khurdadhbih (mid-ninth century) describes these merchants as 'a sort of European (*Saqalibah*), bringing beaver-skins and black fox fur and swords from the furthest parts of their land down to the Black Sea. The Greek Emperor charges tithe on their goods, and if they come down the Don passing Khamlij, the capital of the Khazars, their prince also takes his tithe. They reach the Caspian and take ship again. Some-times they bring their wares by camel from Jurjan to Bagdad, where Slavonic eunuchs interpret for them. They say they are Christian, and pay taxes as such.' The rough Scandinavian with his camel-train in the elegance of Baghdad was very far from Ohthere's ship doubling North Cape, but the same trade had drawn both; though we must not allow the high value which the ninth century set on good furs as luxury articles to make us exaggerate the importance of the Vikings in world trade. But the trade in furs, honey, wax, tar, weapons and slaves enabled a further stock-in-trade to be bought in the Volga delta to supplement the old one, and it was with some new wares that Scandinavian merchants, as professional traders and not simply exporters, arrived in the great international emporium of Jurjan.

At the end of the ninth century we first hear of plundering raids as well. From 910 to 912 a fleet of sixteen ships crossed

the Caspian and attacked Abaskun, killing many of its Mos-
lems. In 912, according to al-Masudi, who certainly exaggerates, the Vikings returned with five hundred ships each with a
hundred men. The Khazars of Atil were in a position to prevent them coming down the Volga, but in return for a promised
half-share of the booty loosed them upon the Caspian. After
taking Baku—its petroleum resources were already known—
they penetrated into Azerbaijan more than three days' march
from the coast. They were eventually defeated, and those who
escaped were later killed on their way back up the Volga.
Al-Masudi said that since then there had been no further
harrying—he was writing in 943, the year of the arrival of
another great raid. Descriptions of this in Ibn Miskawaych
(died 1030) are so detailed that they evidently derive from eye-
witnesses. Whilst the first small raids may have been by new
arrivals down the river-road from the North, it is clear that the
large fleets of the tenth century must have been of Vikings from
Kiev. They had earlier (according to the Nestorian Chronicle)
attacked Constantinople itself in 860, and they did so again
in 941.

In contrast to this traditional scene of sea coasts and river
was the trade-route across the great desert, from Bulgar in the
Volga bend to Khwarizm through Khurasan, and eventually
to China. Silver from the Eastern Caliphate came to Bulgar to
buy the products of this trade, and many arabic *dirhems* minted
in the East may have come by this route to Scandinavian
hoards. The occasional graves of the upper Volga may represent accidental deaths on trading trips, but in the leafy landscape
reminiscent of mid-Sweden which is typical of the Jaroslav
and Vladimir districts small cemeteries are found which must
represent established communities. Some of the graves from the
tenth century and perhaps the very beginning of the eleventh,
contain Scandinavian and Finnish material. If one were to be
confined to archaeological finds one could have no idea that

the Scandinavian journeys along the Volga had reached beyond Bulgar, for outside what might be called the settled production area of their eastern expansion the chances of discovery of the isolated grave of a merchant who died on his travels are small.

There were two main routes to the great centres of Novgorod and Kiev. The first was that southwards from Lake Ladoga, past Staraja Ladoga, down the Volkhov to Novgorod, thence across Lake Ilmen and up the Lovat, Usivat and Kasplja until the boats could be dragged overland to the Dnieper west of Smolensk. The other was to reach this crossing point up the Düna, passing the walls of the fortified (but four times burnt) town of Dünaburg (Daugmaleburg) which was placed at the most difficult part of the navigation and commanded the pas-sage. Archaeological finds of the ninth century seem to group themselves to some extent along the river's course (though not in its upper course where it flowed between steep and inacces-sible banks).

NOVGOROD Novgorod was as important as Kiev to the Scandinavians in Russia. According to the Nestorian Chronicle it was in 862 that Rurik and the first Scandinavians settled there on the Volkhov north of Lake Ilmen. 'From the time of these Varangians the country of Novgorod has been the land of the Rus. The people of Novgorod are now (i.e. when the chronicle was written, in the early twelfth century) of Varangian race, but earlier they were Slavs.' Constantine Porphyrogenitos in his *De Adminis-trando Imperio* (about A.D. 950) writes that, 'the vessels which come to Constantinople from Further Russia are from Nov-gorod where Prince Svjatoslav of the Rus, Igor's son, has his seat.' This is the Igor who had in 941 attacked Constantinople, and the existence of Scandinavian rulers of Novgorod is thus well authenticated: the population was no doubt mainly Slavonic.

Fig. 18 Recent excavations enable one to follow the development of Novgorod from 900 onwards. A winding main street and a

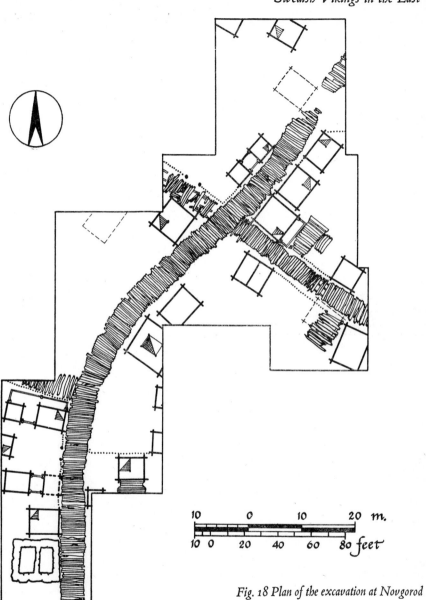

10   0   10   20 m.
10 0   20   40   60   80 feet

Fig. 18 Plan of the excavation at Novgorod

narrow cross street preserved the same alignment until about 1600, though new plank surfaces were laid as the old roads became too muddy. Many finds (including many Slavonic inscriptions on fragments of birch-bark) give us a clear idea of the town's life: it evidently possessed a school, though the pupils drew funny faces as well as letters on their birch-bark 'slates'. Not much of the material is Scandinavian, an oval brooch of the tenth century and some ring-brooches being all that show contact with Scandinavia. It may be that more will be found on the east bank, where it is known the later mer-chants' quarter was.

KIEV

Kiev stood on the steep west bank of the Dnieper, which is not particularly broad at this point, only about half a mile, except in the spring floods when it may be 6 miles wide. A fortnight after the breaking-up of the ice the flood of melting snow arrives and lasts for about six weeks. Mid-April has the highest water level, 6 feet above normal, and Constantine tells us that the Scandinavian merchants gathered in early summer, leaving on their voyage to Byzantium in June while the river was still slightly, but not dangerously, above normal level. The speed of the Dnieper current at Kiev is only one-third that of the Volga, but at Katerinoslav the river has cut its way through granite, the banks are pressed together and it roars through the Dnieper rapids which had each its Scandinavian as well as its Slavonic name. The water-level was higher then, so that the passage may have been somewhat easier than it is now, but beyond the rapids the lowered speed of the current produces many sand bars equally dangerous to navigation until the maze of channels of the delta is reached.

The eighteenth chapter of the Nestorian Chronicle has the title 'Kiev becomes the capital of the Varangians' and dates the event to 882. The story is a fairy-tale of the cunning of King Oleg (of Rurik's line) against two brothers, Askold and Dir, but is followed by a laconic chapter evidently based on annals.

0 1 2 3 4 5 cm

Fig. 19 Scandinavian sword from the Gnezdovo cemetery

In 883 Oleg conquered and taxed the Drevlians, at one black marten fur each. In 884 he conquered the Severians and laid a light tax upon them. He did not permit them to pay tribute to the Khazars for he said, 'I am their enemy.' In 885 he sent envoys to the Radimichians asking, 'To whom do you pay tribute?' They answered, 'To the Khazars.' Oleg said to them, 'You shall not pay tribute to the Khazars but to me.' And they gave Oleg a shilling each, the same as they paid to the Khazars.

99

Constantine Porphyrogenitos follows his account of the gathering of the merchants at Kiev with their ships by a descrip/ tion of their life. 'The hard life of these Rus during the winter is as follows. At the beginning of November the Rus and all their chieftains leave Kiev and go out on *poliudie*, which means their rounds, to the Slavonic regions of the Vervians and Dregovichians and Krivichians and Severians and the rest of the Slavs who pay them tribute. There they are maintained until the departure of the ice in April, when they return to Kiev, fit out their ships, and come down to Romania (the Eastern Empire).' Though this describes the situation in 950, before the Varangian warrior kingdoms were fully developed, a fair number of Scandinavians must have been needed for such an organized collection of tribute. Constantine tells us that boats came from Smolensk, Tjernigov, Teliutza and Busegrad as well as Kiev, and from the two former excavation has revealed much Scandinavian material mainly from the tenth century. West of the present site of Smolensk, on the Dnieper's north bank at Gnezdovo, is a cemetery and two earth ramparts. There are no less than 347 similar defended settlements in the district of Smolensk, a good guide to the turbulent state of affairs in the period. There are four thousand grave/mounds at Gnezdovo, and the six hundred which have been excavated, particularly the richer ones, contain much typical mid/Swedish material, above all weapons, amongst the Byzantine goods which were derived from trade.

Fig. 19

Tjernigov is on the river Dessna, south of Smolensk, and here also there are many graves, some in timbered chambers reminis/ cent of those in Birka, with which they have been compared by T. J. Arne. They provide a good illustration of Ibn Rustah's description of a Swedish chief's burial in Russia: 'When one of their chiefs dies, they dig for him a grave like a roomy house, and lay him in it. They put in his clothes, gold arm/rings, food, jugs of liquor and coins. They also put in the woman he loved, still living, and close the door of the grave, and she dies.' It is striking that, while weapons and belt-mountings are often Scandinavian in taste, the women in the double graves never have any Scandinavian brooches: they were presumably local.

In Kiev archaeological evidence for Scandinavian settlement before the tenth century is lacking. The raid on Constantinople in 860 may have been carried out with a Viking fleet in the Western Mediterranean and not from Kiev, or possibly the earlier cemetery at Kiev has not yet been found. But it is curious that the multitude of burials, both cremation and inhumation, from the tenth and eleventh centuries, should not include any earlier ones if Scandinavian settlement in Kiev really dated from before 860. Only one of the cremation graves, a double one in which man and woman had been burnt together, is very richly furnished, but many of the inhumation burials show close resemblances to mid-Swedish ones of the tenth century. Under the church built by Vladimir on his baptism in 988 are many wooden chamber tombs, containing war-horse as well as warrior. Some of the weapons are purely Scandinavian types: the double-edged sword, the spear, and the long knife carried in the left hand. The axe on the other hand is eastern in type, as in many other Viking graves in Russia. The light, short-hafted axe perhaps seemed more practicable than the heavy northern one, so that they adopted it along with the high, pointed Slavonic iron helmet.

A treaty included in the Nestorian Chronicle (under the date 912) begins, 'We of the Rus: Karl, Ingeld, Farlof, Vermud, Rulov, Gody, Ruald, Karn, Frelav, Aktevu, Truan, Lidul, Fost, Stemid, sent by Oleg, great prince of the Rus and all his subjects, illustrious and mighty princes and by his honourable boyars, to You, Leon and Alexander, great rulers by the grace of God, Emperors of the Greeks, to maintain and strengthen the ancient friendship between the Christians and the Rus.' The ten points which follow are legal agreements about procedure in the case of open killing, murder, theft, in/heritance, ransom of prisoners, stranded ships, etc., reminiscent of the similar arrangements necessitated at this period by like circumstances on the borders of the Danelaw in England. They do not mention the Varangians' right to free baths, free meat, fish, bread and wine, fruit and equipment for their ships, referred to by the Chronicle in 907. Of the ambassadors, not one has a Slavonic name: those that are not Norse are Finnish, and it may be that the document refers not to Kiev but to a state further north, perhaps Novgorod.

According to the Chronicle, Igor attacked Constantinople (with ten thousand ships!) in 941 and was repulsed only at its very walls by Greek fire. He returned in 944 with 'innumerable' ships and this time in proper saga style the Emperor offered him the taxes Oleg had received and more, and Igor with much silk and gold returned to Kiev. The agreement between them was mainly concerned, like that of 912, with legal procedures, but includes three sections on the benefits to be expected by the Rus on their trading voyages to Constantinople. They were to receive free victualling for a month, as well as provisions and equipment for their return journey; but they were not to carry weapons in Constantinople, could only buy silk up to 50 gold pieces worth, and must have it stamped by the Customs on departure. The names of the signatories are mainly Slavonic, though some pure Norse ones are included.

The Nestorian Chronicle is at pains to connect the princely house of Kiev with Rurik, who died in 870 whilst his son Igor was still a minor. Igor in 903 married Olga, and in 942 when Igor must have been about 75 and Olga 60, their son Sviatoslav was born. No events of Igor's reign are recorded after 920 until his alleged raid on Constantinople in 941, and death in 945 whilst demanding taxes from the Drevlians. One may suspect some lacuna in the family/tree at this point.

Olga took over the kingdom on Igor's death. She is described by the Chronicle as 'shining like the moon at night, a pearl among unbelieving rubbish', no doubt because of her conver/ sion to Christianity. Her visit to Constantinople is recorded not only by the Chronicle but by the Emperor Constantine him/ self, and the scale of the ceremonial in his account makes it clear that the Kiev kingdom was a force to be reckoned with. Her beauty and wisdom so captivated Constantine (according to the Chronicle account, not his) that he told her that she should share the throne of the Empire with him. She replied, 'I am heathen: but if you would have me baptized, then bap/ tize me, for I will accept it from no one else.' After her instruc/ tion and baptism Constantine wished to make her his wife. 'But how can I be your wife?' she replied, 'As you have your/ self baptized me, you called me "daughter" and your Christian law does not permit you to marry your daughter, you must know that.' 'Olga, you have tricked me!' Constantine is sup/ posed to have admitted, but gave her rich gifts of gold, silver and silk.

Olga's son Sviatoslav refused to adopt Christianity, ruling with her until 962, and then alone until 972 when he was killed. He was a fierce warrior, plundering the Bulgars of the Danube as well as of the Volga, and the Khazars. The Chronicle says that he took no baggage, even cooking/pots, on his expeditions, and would have no meat except strips that had been roasted on the embers, and no tent but his saddle over his head. The Byzantine historian Leo Diaconus saw Sviatos/ lav when he signed a treaty with the Emperor Johannes Tzimiskes in 971, on the Danube, and left the following des/ cription of him. 'He came across the river in a Scythian boat, rowing with his men. He was of medium height, broad/ shouldered with a long and luxurious moustache. His nose was stubby, eyes blue and eyebrows bushy, and his head was shaven apart from a lock on one side which was a sign of nobility. In one ear was a gold ring with two pearls and a ruby between them: his white gown differed from his men's only by being cleaner: he appeared brooding and wild.' The description has many features (the hair lock, *osolodets*, in particular) of the Cossack *hetman* of the sixteenth century, and suggests how quickly the Rus were becoming Slavonic. Sviatoslav is not a Scandinavian name, and it is probable that he was in part of Slavonic descent. After his death a struggle for power broke out between his three sons, Oleg, Jaropolk and Vladimir. It ended about 980 when Vladimir triumphed after the other two had been killed. He was a strong ruler, who strengthened and extended the rule of Kiev.

In 988 Vladimir was converted to Christianity; he is compared by the Chronicle with Solomon. Vladimir is said to have had three hundred concubines in Vyshgorod, the same number in Bjelogorod and two hundred in Berestov, whereas Solomon was credited with seven hundred wives and three hundred concubines. The chronicler adds, 'Vladimir was foolish, but found redemption in the end: Solomon was wise, but erred at last.' After his baptism, Vladimir systematically christianized the Rus, and built churches not only in Kiev but throughout his lands. He established the firm and quite characteristic structure of Kiev, a city-state with an economic system much more like the Byzantine one and that of late antiquity than the feudal system of Europe. It is quite possible that he and the other Rus princes dreamt of founding a commercial empire, but the influence of Byzantium certainly became ever stronger in Kiev, in economic as well as in cultural matters. In spite of this Kiev retained a certain individuality, and one must not forget that in many respects it went its own way: neither in religion nor in art did it slavishly follow Byzantium. Its Church used Slavonic and not Greek as its language, and this was very important in encouraging independent development.

During the tenth century Byzantium was certainly the dominant influence on the culture of Kiev: there the Rus made contact with a world of richness and luxury which must have seemed immensely impressive to them. When the Varangian bodyguard in Constantinople began to be largely recruited from men of good family from Scandinavia and England, the links between the Rus and Byzantium were naturally strength, ened. This was in the early eleventh century, and though the contacts were occasionally hostile, they were so only for short periods. For without Byzantium, Kiev could not survive, and it was through Kiev that Byzantine culture exerted a growing influence upon the Slavonic peoples, and became one of the foundations of the development in later centuries of Russia.

The prince who from many points of view, literary, juridical and social, meant most for the development of Kiev was Vladimir's son Jaroslav. After bloody fraternal strife he became ruler in 1019 and died in 1054. The list of his relations by marriage gives an impressive indication of the importance of the Rus kingdom at this date. He married Ingegerd the daughter of Olaf Skotkonung, and became the father-in-law of Harald Hardradi of Norway, Andrew I of Hungary and Henry I of France.

CHAPTER V

Iceland, Greenland and America

THE EARLY DEVELOPMENT of historical scholarship in Iceland means that we are better informed about this part of the Viking expansion than any other. *Landnámabók*, the history of the settlement of Iceland, tracing the prominent families of the thirteenth century back to their founding fathers of the ninth, explicitly refers to Bede's *Ecclesiastical History* as an authority. Ari the Wise (1067–1148) tells us that Iceland was inhabited by Christians when the first Scandinavians arrived. The Christians went away, because they did not wish to live alongside heathens, leaving books, bells and croziers from which one could tell that they were Irish. Four Roman coins of the late third century, found in two different places in Iceland, suggest that people from Scotland visited the island about A.D. 300.

ICELAND The discoverers of Iceland were, traditionally, two: Gardar, a Swede who was blown off his course on his way to the Hebrides, and Naddod, a Norwegian living in Færoe who was on his way home to Norway. The story of these two weather-beaten navigators need not be implicitly believed; it is typical of the sagas to dramatize in such terms the growth of settlement in Iceland. It is more likely prosaic fact that the populations of the western islands who had for a long time known and visited Iceland showed Vikings the way thither. The first planned expedition was led by Floki Vilgerðarson from Rogaland. He went by way of Shetland and Færoe with two ships and wintered in Iceland. The first real settlement was that of Ingolfr Arnarson who took women and children and farm stock with him, traditionally in the twelfth year of Harald Harfagri's reign. The main emigration covered the two generations round A.D. 900. *Landnámabók* gives us the names of over three thousand people (probably twice as many left Norway in these years) and of 1,400 places. Brøgger has pointed out that at least half of those who can be localized come from the Gulatingslag, the Hardanger-Voss-Sogn area of Norway. This, taken with the Icelandic tradition that the emigrants were those who had refused to accept Harald's sovereignty, would seem to connect the settlement with Harald's establishment of his authority in western Norway. Others came from the Atlantic Islands and a few from Britain.

The men who went to Iceland had had a position indepen-dent of the king, and whilst certainly other factors, such as the need for new lands, played their part, one gets the impression from accounts of Icelandic life in the sagas that a reaction against the new concept of the State was a powerful force. The organization of the Icelandic republic of the tenth century as an almost completely free State was possible only because there was no risk of war with any enemy. There were no natives who might (as in England or France) attempt to reconquer their land, and no immediate likelihood of the sort of Viking raids which afflicted other countries.

A comparison of the Icelandic basic law with the Norwegian from which it was taken is illuminating, for it shows a pre-sumably deliberate step back from even the rudimentary ideas of the State accepted in Norwegian traditional law before Harald's centralizing enterprise. The legislature, judicature and executive were completely separated, and it seems from the sagas that there was a reluctance to admit even the authority represented by the exercise of the judgment of an individual upon the facts of a case. In many cases in the sagas the decision in a lawsuit depends entirely upon what must seem to us extremely narrow technicalities, without any regard to the justice of the cause. In a republic of such fierce individualists this may have been inevitable. When judgment had been recurred, it was left to the aggrieved party to carry out the sentence—if he could.

The legal code is credited by tradition to Ulfljot who took it from the *Gulatingslag*, and it was accepted by the *Alþingi c.* 930. The island was divided into twelve legal districts each with three *goðar*: later, in order to provide a court of appeal, three more *goðar* were established. The *goðar* formed the *lǫgretta* which appointed the *lǫgsǫumaðr* who was as it were the Speaker of the *Alþingi*. The *goði* combined secular, religious, economic and judicial power: he was the representative and helper of his 'friends' *vis-à-vis* other men and the gods, and decided questions at issue between them. But his authority over them was ill-defined, and if they felt he did not support them energetically enough, or was unjust, they could transfer their allegiance to another *goði*. With this structure of society it is not surprising that developments in Iceland were unlike those in Norway or any other country. It made an independent critical interest in affairs, and minute interest in family connections, more natural than among the powerless lay peasantry of other lands, and provided the foundation for one of the greatest artistic achievements of the Viking peoples, the Icelandic Sagas.

The centre of Iceland is a lava desert and the population was dependent on sheep-farming, fishing and fowling rather than arable land. Much use was made of summer-pastures (the *saeter* system of husbandry) and settlement was scattered. The horse was therefore more important in Iceland than elsewhere in Scandinavia where coastal sea-traffic is much easier. Though trees were more plentiful then than now (when they are confined to two or three small areas) timber was always scarce and driftwood was carefully collected. Most houses were built of stone and turf, and have therefore left more traces than wooden ones. Those in *Þjórsárdalr* which were overwhelmed by the eruption of Hekla in July 1300 were excavated by a Scandinavian expedition in 1939. Skallakot is a typical example of the period of the Settlement, a hall about 84 feet long, with slightly curved walls. A long 8-foot hearth occupied the middle of the building, which was divided into four rooms. Three small, square store-rooms were later built on to the north wall. It is typical of the stone and turf building tradition of the treeless districts of south-west Norway, Rogaland and West Agder.

Iceland remained heathen until the decision to accept Christianity was taken by the Althing in A.D. 1000; one might expect therefore at least thirty-nine temple-sites (one for each *goði*). In fact not one certain example is known (that often quoted, Hofstaðir in Myvatn, is a farm) and it has even been doubted whether temples, in spite of the saga references to them, really existed in Iceland. Before the acceptance of Christianity, the dead had been buried in heathen fashion but they were not burnt. This may have been because the influences from the British Isles were stronger than *Landnámabók* (which does mention some settlers from the British Isles) believed. There are one hundred and twenty-three known archaeological sites in Iceland with two hundred and forty-six graves, mainly along the rivers on the north coast. The graves, mainly tenth-century, are on the whole inconspicuous, sometimes unmarked, usually containing coffins and only occasionally boats. It is curious, when one remembers how characteristic the Icelandic contribution to literature was, that the clothes, weapons and ornaments from the graves should be so indistinguishable from those of other Scandinavians. As might be expected, they resemble most closely those of Norway, with some south-eastern (perhaps Swedish) elements. The trading wares and imports so common elsewhere are strikingly absent in Iceland, even the common soapstone bowls. A niello-inlaid southern English sword from Knafahólum, and a sword blade of Continental origin with the Ulfbrht stamp, are the only imported weapons, one or two Scottish ring brooches the only ornaments, to show contacts with other than Scandinavian countries. Was this apparent isolation real? It appears from the sagas that the leading families travelled extensively and had good contacts abroad, but one can only say from the archaeological evidence that this does not appear to have affected the mass of the people. This absence of concern with developments abroad may indeed have been one of the conditions for the production of the sagas, almost a national introspection.

After some generations the Icelanders felt themselves to be Icelanders rather than Norwegians, and their interest in their own history strengthened, genealogical sagas accumulating round their great families. One of the liveliest and most distinc‑ tive forms of the literature of the European Middle Ages thus developed on this distant island on the fringes of the Arctic circle.

GREENLAND   Greenland is almost 200 miles from Iceland, but the moun‑
Plate 44   tains of both are so high that half‑way across one can still see Snæfellsness in Iceland and the summits of Angmagssalik in Greenland. According to tradition it was about A.D. 900 that Gunnbjörn was driven by the wind to 'Gunnbjörns skerries' (off the east coast of Greenland), and it is surprising that there was a delay of three generations before Icelanders went there. The founder of the first colony (and real discoverer of Green‑ land) was Erik the Red. His father had been expelled from Norway for killing, and Erik in his turn for the same cause from Iceland. He sailed along the inhospitable east coast, round Cape Farewell, and wintered on Erik's island. In spring he sailed up the fjord (Tunugdliarfik) to the most fertile part of Greenland, and on his return to Iceland recommended his new field of settlement with a good name, Greenland, as opposed to Iceland. In 986, twenty‑five ships laden with emigrants and cattle sailed for Greenland; only fourteen arrived. Erik chose the best spot in the fjord for his farm Brattahlið (Steep slope), which became the centre of the first colony. After ten years the area (modern Julianehaab) was well settled and another colony was established further north in the present‑day Godthaab,

known as the western settlement, Vestribygð. The original one was known as Eystribygð: both were in fact on the west coast, and the southern one, Eystribygð, was in about the latitude of Bergen, further south than Iceland. The influence of the Gulf Stream, which gave a comparatively mild climate in Iceland and Norway, was lacking, and they had the cold Greenland current instead.

Nowadays Eriksfjord is frozen from October to May, and whilst the climate may have been milder then, it must have been a hard life. There is archaeological evidence that some corn-growing was tried, but animal husbandry was the main resource, and bones of cattle, sheep, goats and pigs have been found. The produce of the chase (whale, seal, fish, bear, reindeer) was very important for food, and walrus-ivory and polar-bear skins as valuable exports were needed to purchase corn and iron. There is some trace of a native iron-working industry, but it is very late, and most iron must have been imported. The farm-houses of stone and turf have survived *Fig. 20* better than in Iceland, and are to be found all over the areas of ancient settlement. The corridor-type with rooms opening off a long passage is later than Erik's day; it was not introduced into Iceland and Greenland until the twelfth century. It is striking that the frequent church ruins in Greenland are evidently modelled on those of the Scottish islands, and not of the usual Icelandic form. Only the first period of the settlement (for which we have only literary sources) belongs to the Viking Age, and that to the end of it. The pathetic later story, for which we have a wealth of archaeological evidence, is part of the history of medieval Scandinavia.

It is no great distance from the Icelandic settlements in Green- AMERICA land to America, much less than the direct passage from Bergen to Greenland which the sea-going *hafskip* quite usually took. No permanent settlement was ever established, for it was not a matter of occupying an uninhabited land, but of conquering

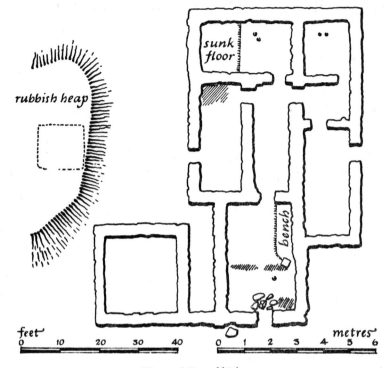

Fig. 20 A Brattahlið house

one by force, and for this the colonists did not have sufficient numbers. Nevertheless the Vinland voyage was for some time the great adventure for the Greenlanders, and their dream was of the colonization of a rich new country. The stories of these voyages were handed down from generation to generation until they were recorded, probably about 1200. We have such accounts in two sagas, the *Eriks saga rauða* (in *Hauksbók*) and *Groenlendinga saga* (in *Flateyjarbók*), which is rather more reliable. The details must naturally have been subject to some change during the long transmission, and the stories are not to be relied on in detail. Such details as the wild grapes of Vinland making a man drunk are evidently improvements on the original, but the general point, that some Viking voyagers reached the shores of North America, is certain. Unfortunately the archaeological evidence which has been used to support this has been either contrived or mistaken.

On a voyage from Iceland to Greenland, Bjarni Herjulfsson, three days out, became fogbound and made landfall on a flat and wooded land which he did not think could be Greenland. He put about and after two days made another landfall which was also not Greenland. Three days later he sighted a rocky and inhospitable land which, after coasting round it, he found to be an island and not Greenland. Four days later, having refused to accept any substitutes, Bjarni and his crew arrived in Greenland. It is difficult to understand how this dry and disinterested account of an obviously cautious if rather narrow-minded seaman can ever have seemed to merit dismissal as a fantastic legendary claim. It is interesting to note that contemporaries on his return to Norway thought that he had shown very little curiosity about his new lands.

In 986 Leif Eriksson (son of the founder of the Greenland colony) bought Bjarni's ship (which one may imagine was a good reliable example of the *hafskip* type) and set out with a crew of thirty-five to rediscover these lands. The fact that he was able to repeat Bjarni's landfalls in the opposite order suggests that Bjarni knew fairly well where he had been, and had, after the first fog lifted, been winning his way consistently back to Greenland though unaware that various land masses intervened. The rocky coast was called Helluland, or 'stone land', the wooded one Markland or 'forest land'. Eventually they wintered further south in a fjord where there were salmon bigger than those in Greenland and the grass grew all winter. They also found grapes. How much further south this was has given rise to much discussion. At the present time, salmon are not found south of 41° N. on the American coast. Vines are not found north of 42° N. If we assume that Leif's astronomical observation that 'the sun was above the horizon at the *eykt* point and the *dagmal* point' means an amplitude of S. 60 W. (which is probably the best solution of a highly technical piece of Viking navigation), this would correspond to a latitude of 37° N.—Chesapeake Bay on the Virginian coast. An error of only fourteen minutes in time (either on Leif's part, or on ours in our understanding of *eykt*) alters the position 4° to the north-ward, and it therefore seems best to conclude that Vinland may have been somewhere near Boston.

On Leif's return to Greenland his brother Thorvald's interest was aroused. Bjarni's ship was prepared for yet another voyage to Vinland under a third owner, this time with a crew of thirty. It is perhaps an indication that the position of Vinland was now satisfactorily plotted (and that there was nothing unusual in this) that Thorvald sailed direct to Vinland and the saga does not comment on it. They lived there for two years, until Thorvald was killed after the first contact with the 'Skraelings' or natives. He was buried here and one cross was erected at his head and another at his feet. It is clear that his intention was to settle in Vinland; previous expeditions had not met any inhabi-tants. His men returned to Greenland, and the old ship that had carried Bjarni, Leif, and Thorvald to Vinland was fitted out again for its last Vinland voyage under Thorsteinn, an unsuccessful attempt to recover his brother Thorvald's body. In the event they returned after a summer's wandering over the sea without even having found Vinland.

The next expedition to Vinland we hear of in the sources is the largest of all, an attempt to find new land and colonize this remote area. The leader was Thorfinn Karlsefni, an Ice-lander from Reynines in Skagafjord. He sailed with two ships (with forty men in each) to Eriksfjord in Greenland one sum-mer, and married the beautiful Gudrid, a second-generation immigrant from Iceland. During the winter in which they

were married there was a good deal of talk in Greenland con-
cerning Vinland the Good, and in summer they fitted out three
ships, and with a hundred and sixty men followed Leif
Eriksson's route west. The saga tells of a large dark champion
called Thorhall (and cites some verses by him) who accompanied Thorfinn to Helluland and Markland, but left him at
Straumfjord and sailed back, whilst Thorfinn continued to
the southward. After much sailing they came to the mouth of a
river which formed a lake and then flowed into the sea. Outside
the mouth lay large islands which meant that they could only
enter the river at high water. When they sailed up the river
they found fertile land, with wild corn and grapes, and the
rivers full of fish. They had only to dig holes in the beach
where they would be covered at high tide, to catch halibut in
them at low water. They stayed there a month: the woods were
rich in game, and they had their own cattle with them.

One morning they saw nine skin boats; the men on board
were waving rods. It was clearly a peaceful visit, and the
Scandinavians went towards them with white shields as a
token of peace, and the men who were small and ugly, with
unkempt hair, large eyes and broad cheeks, came ashore. They
stayed a little time, appearing very surprised, and then rowed
away.

The winter was mild, and the cattle could be left out at
pasture. Early in spring a whole fleet of the skin boats arrived,
and trading began between the Scandinavians and the Indians,
who were eager to buy red cloth in exchange for furs. Karlsefni
forbade any sale of swords or spears to the Indians. As supplies
ran shorter trade continued lively, and the cloth was cut up
into even smaller portions. One is bound to be reminded of the
Scandinavian merchants in the Near East (though there they
had been the sellers of furs) trading with the Arabs for strips of
silk. Unfortunately one of Karlsefni's oxen rushed bellowing
out of the wood, and the Indians took it as a bad omen and

disappeared. After three days they appeared in large numbers waving their staves, and Karlsefni's men took red shields and went towards them. There was a battle, and the saga describes with great clarity the Indian habit of using a long stave with, fastened to the end of it, a stone in a pig's stomach, with which to strike the enemy. This weapon we know to have been used later by the Algonquin Indians of New England, who called it a 'devil's head'. If the stone was sewn into a fresh skin it was firmly anchored to the stave as the tissue dried, and was then painted with terrifying faces. For throwing, or striking, at skin boats it must have been an effective weapon.

The settlers realized that they would never be able to establish themselves in Vinland, and retreated to Straumfjord where they spent the third winter, and then returned to Greenland. It was natural in the isolated and uneventful Greenland community that Karlsefni's great expedition of one hundred and sixty men to Vinland should be the great adventure about which its participants must have had many opportunities to recite dramatic tales. When the saga was written down the events will not have lost anything in the telling, and it is clear that in its present form it has drawn upon many differing narrators. But there can be no doubt that at any rate the main outline is true enough, though some minor details are obviously false. It is a real saga of a 'land-taking', perhaps the most dramatic in the whole of Norse literature, but unfortunately it scarcely helps us to determine Vinland's exact position. The details of the wild corn, the vines, the mild winter, and others, may well be taken directly from Leif Eriksson's account of Vinland. But others, the meeting with the Indians, their manner of fighting, and the Scandinavians' retreat, give the impression of genuine experience. There are some internal contradictions (the detail of the winter pasture and references to the next summer go oddly with the evident impression the saga's later parts give that Karlsefni was only a few months in the South, and that he never wintered there) that suggest how different travellers' differing accounts have been melted down to make the artistic whole which Karlsefni's saga now presents.

Karlsefni's voyage was certainly not the last to Vinland and Markland. In many sources we find more or less incidental references to Vinland and the well-wooded Markland. The Icelandic annals tell us that the bishop of Greenland, Erik Gnúpsson, went to seek Vinland in 1121, but evidently never returned. Perhaps he went as a missionary to the Skrælings: his visit shows that knowledge of Vinland still survived, naturally enough, a century after Leif Eriksson. If there was any thought then of colonizing Vinland it was too late, for the conditions for colonization were past. But without leaving any traces in history, the Greenlanders may have continued to provide them-selves with timber from Markland, which lay so much nearer than Norway. The coffins at Herjulfsnes are made of large planks of pine, deal and larch, and the larch certainly cannot have come from Norway. One may of course assume it to be driftwood, but at a time when regular voyages were made be-tween Greenland and Europe it seems more likely that the comparatively short trip to Markland was often made.

CHAPTER VI

The Art of the Viking Age

O UR KNOWLEDGE of Viking art is still very incomplete.
We have numerous weapons, ornaments and other objects,
most of metal but some of wood, which give us an idea of the
art and craft of the period. But there are very few monuments
which give us a real understanding of the taste and artists of

Fig. 21 the times. The Oseberg find is one of these, the more important
because it belongs to a transition between old and new and
shows the emergence of what was to remain the dominant
strain in Viking art. The group of court artists of the early ninth
century who were engaged upon it, called by Shetelig in his
masterly analysis 'the Vestfold school', included representatives
of the old Vendel style like the 'Academician' who carved the
animal-head post and the sledge shaft, or the other man who
was responsible for the ship's stem and sternposts. The strength

Plate 45 and elegance of the lion's head, tautly erect on the tense neck,
make it one of the masterpieces of Viking art. The Academician disciplines it into a whole by keeping to the original surface
in his design and cutting away the parts in between the ornament, instead of carrying out the ornament in relief. The neck
may have been meant for painting, as it is plain with the
exception of an unfinished field of squares and roundels at the
bottom, or perhaps the artist, whose taste was that of a past
generation, died without finishing his work.

The 'Master of the Prow' is at once freer and more forceful in
style, perhaps because he has to cover long narrow fields. This
is not to imply that the Academician is boring: his ornament

Fig. 22 based always on birds is only superficially symmetrical, never
completely and mechanically so, and whilst he worked in the
old Vendel style he had evidently been influenced by themes
from the British Isles. It is rather that the Master of the Prow

118

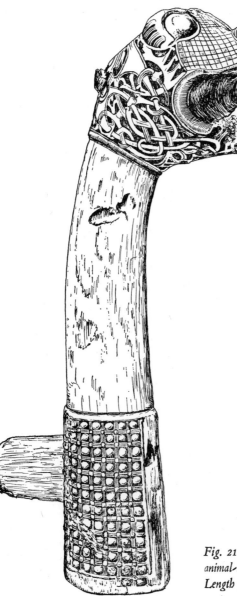

Fig. 21 *The Academician's animal-head post, Oseberg. Length 52 cm.*

Fig. 22 Detail of the Academician's sledge pole, Oseberg

Fig. 23

Fig. 24

lacks the Academician's elegant manipulation of line, and leaves whole areas of his animals' bodies as flat surfaces. They are the usual ornamental quadrupeds, but on the inside of the prow he also used the human figure, which one meets from time to time in the art of the Migration and Vendel periods. Uppermost on it we see three glassy-eyed bothered-looking gentlemen, who have retained their human shape. Lower down they have become more animal-like and their hands grip the limbs, beards or hair of their neighbours. These, particularly the gripping men, represent the new currents which gave rise to the Oseberg style. We cannot call the Master of the Prow their inventor, for he uses them only occasionally and by and large adheres to the older style. He does not, for instance, use the strap-work framework which was one of the characteristic features of the new style.

Perhaps the oldest of the objects in the Oseberg find is 'Shetelig's sledge'. There are three richly ornamented sledges and one plain working one, each fitted with a detachable frame (like that on a hay-wain) to hold the cargo. These frames do not belong to the sledges they are placed on: the burial took place in summer, and it seems that these pieces were taken from the store-shed just as they came to hand. Each corner of Shetelig's sledge is ornamented with a wild lion's head, a copy only slightly worked-over of the classical lion's head of contemporary Continental art. The sides of the sledge body are divided up by mouldings in two different planes, with under them a third level of the older animal ornament related to that of the Academician and the Master of the Prow. It was originally painted (traces were found during excavation) but only in black, and represents the school very well in that it has two motifs from Carolingian art and one (the animal ornament) of traditional pattern. On the sledge, the union of these is not particularly skilful.

Plate 49

Fig. 25

The Carolingian animal-head post is a good example of the successful blend that was the developed Oseberg style. The surface is divided by a framework of strap-work and in its

Fig. 26

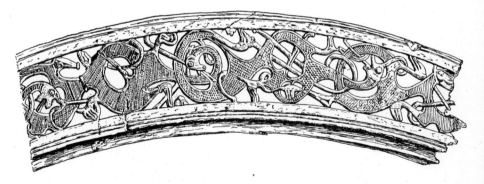

Fig. 23 Decoration from the prow of the Oseberg ship

Plate 46

Plate 47

*Fig. 24 Decor-
ation from the
inside of the
Oseberg stem*

roundels small animals are clambering, their claws gripping every possible hold. The difference is not merely that the elegance of the old Vendel serpentine ornament has been re-placed by a knotted muscularity, but that the surface has disap-peared in a welter of high relief. One can no longer properly grasp the form of the whole, as one could with the Academi-cian's treatment. The most developed representative of this newer style is called by Shetelig the 'Baroque Master' whose development we may perhaps see in three pieces from Oseberg. In the first animal-head post his confident variations in the basic motif of strap-work, quadrupeds and birds undeniably interfere with any unified over-all impression. In the sledge-shafts his taste is surer, the composition clearer, but in the second animal-head post he has been tempted by his very great accomplishment in technique to overload the work. He must have been one of the influential artists who formed the Viking Age's first independent style, the Oseberg or 'gripping beast' style. It would be wrong to think of him as necessarily a suc-cessor of the Academician: in fact the two pillars done by the Baroque Master are worn by use whereas the Academician's is not (it may of course be unfinished). The possibility of dis-tinguishing the dates of the ten artists represented is very limited. The ship had been in use for some time before its use in the burial, as its worn keel shows; but whereas the ornament above the water line is somewhat weathered, that below the waterline is as fresh as if it had been cut yesterday.

Outside Vestfold the only place in Scandinavia which has produced enough material (small bronzes) to give us an idea of the personality of certain ninth-century artists is Gotland. But the two whose work we find represented in finds from Broa in Halla in the middle of Gotland (perhaps the seat of a great family) are not as dependent upon earlier tradition as the Academician of the Vestfold school, but resemble more the work of the Master of the Prow. The bronze harness-orna-

Fig. 25 The gable-end of Shetelig's sledge, Oseberg

ments bear animals with real bodies instead of the old bands, though they preserve some of the rhythm of line of the earlier style. Some of the mountings are in the shape of a lion's head, others decorated with large animal masks in relief. The division into fields by strap-work is well carried through, and like the Baroque Master of Oseberg the artist's work is characterized by a certain excess of detail. It seems that the artist was used to working on a larger scale, and that he was, if not a practised woodcarver himself (which seems most likely, from some details of surface ornament) a man very eclectic in technique, copying the details of the outstanding woodcarvers of his day. Neither he nor the other artist who made the great bronze brooch could, however, be credited with any decisive role in the development of later taste.

Fig. 27

The ornament on the brooch from Broa is divided between the traditional animals of the preceding style and two new species. The gripping beast is introduced into one or two of the fields into which the surface is divided. The ornament on the back is more personal in style. The Carolingian lions, a feature of the fashionable taste of the day, completely fill the irregularly-shaped surface, and the adaptation of them to this surface gives them fantastic shapes. All that remains of the former style is

Fig. 28

Fig. 26 Detail of the Carolingian animal-head post, Oseberg

the animal-heads. On the back, the artist has covered the end of the brooch with two heraldically disposed birds, whose heads together form a large mask. It is a simple line-drawing without any internal contours to suggest relief, partly using the edge of the brooch for the outline, and the execution is most reminiscent of a manuscript illumination. The man who made the Broa brooch was no great artist, but his work is important

Fig. 27 Lion from a bronze harness-mount. Broa in Halla, Gotland

because it shows so clearly how the proud lion of the Continental style was adopted on Gotland in the early ninth century, and
how it was altered in the process.

Another piece of Gotland work, the sword from Ristimäki
in Finland, is much more elegant than the Broa brooch. It
shows clearly how easy it was to adapt the birds of the Con-   *Fig. 29*
tinental style to the native one, whereas the lion on the whole
retained its original feeling.

The most accomplished piece in this style is a sword-hilt   Plate 55
from Stora Ihre in the parish of Hellvi. Here we find the
majestic lion with a bird's head composed into three roundels
formed in the native style. It is also interesting because of its
stamped pattern-ornament, a technique evidently known only
on Gotland.

These Gotland artists who lived in a period of transition
between old and new were more tied by the old than were those
of the Vestfold school responsible for the new style. They

take up new themes which are in part the same as those of the Vestfold group, but they cannot completely free themselves of the old assumptions, and thus their art represents only a rela-tively brief phase. The new gripping-beast style—the earlier Oseberg style—appears in their work taken over as a direct loan from Oseberg. The Gotland artists made no new contribution to it and did not develop it, and it is thus natural that we should feel something missing in their work by comparison with the Oseberg re-working of foreign themes in a creative way which related them to the native cultural environment.

In the Oseberg wood-carvings, and also in the small bronze objects with gripping beasts, there is an elastic force and almost magic tension which distinguishes them from both their pre-decessor, the Vendel style, and their successors. It has been urged that the Oseberg animal-heads were explicitly intended to be terrifying, that the artists sought deliberately to give ex-pression to the threat of violence. One must recall the provision

Plates 48, 49

of the earliest Icelandic legal code, Ulfljot's law, that ships approaching Iceland should remove the carved figure-head so that it should not frighten away the good guardian spirits of the country. It is scarcely going too far to associate some of the Oseberg heads with a desire to frighten, if not men at any rate evil spirits. There is thus a functional element in the modifica-tion of Carolingian animal ornament which we see in the Oseberg style. For artists working on the large scale of the

Fig. 28 Animal figures from the back of the Broa brooch

Oseberg pieces there can scarcely be any question of influence from such handy small objects as buckles or manuscripts as the sources of inspiration. There must have been direct personal experience in furniture and sculpture, if not of the naturalist animal portrayal of Continental art, at any rate of some simpli-fied version of it in the northern provinces of the Carolingian Empire. The British Isles might also be considered as a source, for the origin of the gripping beast is not yet satisfactorily determined. The beast in itself does not constitute a style but

*Fig. 29 Lion from the
Ristimäki sword, Finland*

merely a motif, and it is illuminating to observe that the master
of the Carolingian animal head-post uses it as it were arbitrarily
to fill the fields, with no systematic grouping. The Baroque
Master is more concerned to adapt it to older traditional arrangements, and to make it the basis of the ornament's organization,
and it was this which was decisive for the style's subsequent
development.

The later ship finds, Gokstad, Tune and Borre, are in a
much more fragmentary condition, but one or two comparisons
enable us to see the line of development. The gable-ends of the
Gokstad ship shelter are descended from the heads on the
Oseberg bed. But they are longer, with large pointed ears and
tense upturned tongue more drawn out. The eyes are quite
round, lacking the little triangle at the corner. That feature was
very common in Irish and northern English art, and suggests
that the master who carved the Oseberg bed and barge-boards
had some connections with that art. Paint must have been as
important in the total effect of the flat animal-heads of Gokstad
as in those of Oseberg. The colours used at Gokstad were black
and yellow, with occasional red. The large animals had an
ornamented band of knotwork round their necks, and its
form echoed the oriental palmette loop.

Figs. 30, 31

127

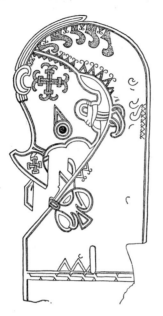

Fig. 30 Carved animal head from the Ose-berg bed. Maximum width 49·4 cm.

Fig. 32

On the tiller of the Gokstad ship we find the same head as on the barge-boards though conceived more in the round. For practical reasons it lacks the peaked ears, which would have got in the way of the helmsman. The large human masks which we find in the Oseberg ornament, for example on the sledge-shaft carved by the Baroque Master, recur at Gokstad in the small boats. They, like the animal-heads on the barge-boards, show a further development, a freer shaping of the lobes of ornament round the masks. Here one can trace a native tradition, but this should not lead one to think of the tenth century, as represented by Gokstad, as more rigorously native in taste. There are for example the two round ornaments, one with a rider, the other with a lion, which though unmistakably Norse products are direct copies of English originals. Theirs is a pure pictorial art, without preoccupation with ornamental pattern, a type which we see represented at Oseberg by the textiles.

Fig. 33

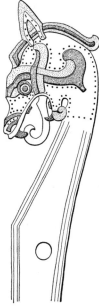

Fig. 31 Carved animal head at the gable-end of the Gokstad ship shelter. Maximum width 38cm.

The style of the royal grave-mounds at Borre, from which it derives its name, with its characteristic twisted ring animal with cat-like head seen full face, and gripping claws, shows a development of the Oseberg style. The flat animal-head of the bridle-bit is of the same family as those on the Oseberg bed. What is new is the combination of the cat-like face with inter-lace ornament in the form of a ring-chain giving rise to triangu-lar fields crossed by triple or quadruple lines. The bands com-posing the interlace have double lines which are cross-hatched, probably to imitate filigree work. From the end of the ninth to the middle of the tenth century this style was very important in Norway and Sweden and to a lesser extent in Denmark, par-ticularly in fairly simple work. It is very unusual to find high-quality material in it. What there is is often heavily influenced by a foreign style. When in the middle of the tenth century or somewhat later the Danish Jellinge style took its final shape it

Fig. 34

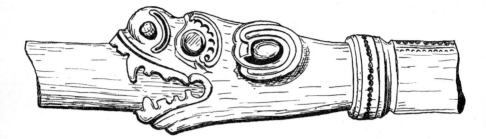

Fig. 32 The tiller of the Gokstad ship. Length of the head to the collar, 19·6 cm.

Fig. 35

was heavily influenced from England, where Scandinavian settlers had developed their own art, the English Jellinge style. Some features of it, the profile head with short muzzle and long lappet, and bands which swell in thickness, are found as early as the Oseberg style and are obviously from Scandinavia. The best pieces in the Borre style with Jellinge features are a gold spur and belt ornament from Röd, by Värne, in Östfold in Norway. The ornament is carried out in true filigree, and a delicate variation in thickness of thread and size of bead emphasizes the pattern, the typical ring-chain with rows of birds' heads in profile. It is in very high relief, reminiscent almost of pierced ornament, which may well derive from the style of the Oseberg Baroque Master.

The collection of small bronze ornaments from the Borre graves is not a large one, but one can see in it individual variations in theme and treatment reminiscent of those at Oseberg, and it is clear that a whole school of artists of differing ideas was involved in their production. The homeland of the style was Norway, and apart from the ring-chain ornament it developed

Fig. 33 Norse ornament from Gokstad, copying an English original

smoothly out of the preceding Oseberg style. It is the strong individual preference of artists working within a style (whether Oseberg or Borre) for particular themes which makes the transition from Borre to Jellinge so unclear. This also explains why the Borre style, when one does find it on high-quality work, appears in so many different guises. The transition be, tween Borre and Jellinge is further obscured by the fact that the northern English styles which were so important a factor in the shaping of the Jellinge style had also for generations influenced the Borre style as well.

Fig. 36

Outside Norway little really good Borre,style work has been found. A round silver brooch from Gärdslösa, on Öland, shows the style in a fairly compact (and somewhat barbaric) form. It is dominated by four large mask,like faces, and between them typical double,ring animals with bodies formed of a ring,knot; round the edges and in between the masks lies a ring,chain pattern; parts are decorated with inlaid ornament in niello. Thus the brooch includes all the features characteristic of the Borre style.

Plate 56

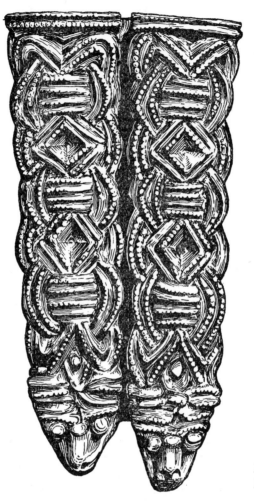

Fig. 34 Straptags from Borre. Length 5·8 cm.

Fig. 37

In the rectangular silver brooches from Ödeshög, in Öster‑ götland (part of a hoard dated by the coins to the middle of the tenth century) the mixture of elements appears clearly. The rings are arranged in a row in the middle and along the short

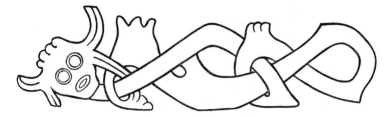

Fig. 35 Decorative figure from Shetelig's sledge, Oseberg

sides, surrounded by strip-animals in an angular plait which is derived directly from Oseberg. The animal-heads are rather stiffly stylized to fit the area. The filigree-work is delicate and related to that on the large silver brooch from Eketorp, in Plates 52, 53, Närke, which is contemporary with it. The style of the Eketorp 54 brooch (and even more that of a contemporaneous triangular silver niello brooch from Östra Herrestad in Skåne in a hoard of about 925) can no longer be considered pure Borre style. Nevertheless, the shaping of the animal-bodies still shows *Fig. 38* the connection with Oseberg, and the band-like bodies which swell and narrow down are a development of older native traditions.

These last two ornaments might be described as part of the tenth-century development leading towards the Jellinge style. What has been preserved is such a small proportion of what must have existed (we have for instance not a single architec- tural fragment, piece of furniture, or work of art of monumental character from Scandinavia in this period) that one cannot hope to follow the stages of this development in detail. In Sweden one can find no trace at this period of any cultural centre with which artists could have been connected and which might have provided the economic conditions conducive to the flourishing of art. One suspects that the merchants of Birka were rather uninterested in native artists: in their graves one

Fig. 36 Twisted ring animal on a buckle from Birka, Björkön

finds a certain amount of good work, but usually on objects brought home from abroad, and it seems that the *nouveau-riche* merchant was usually more concerned with showy adornment than quality.

In the ninth century, as far as we can see from the scanty finds, artists in Denmark had in part borrowed and adapted Carolin-gian elements such as animal and acanthus, in part borrowed ideas from the Vestfold school which may on occasion have produced work to Danish order. The regeneration of Danish art seems to have occurred about, or soon after, the middle of the tenth century, and it is possible that it came from a group of artists who gathered at Harald Bluetooth's court, or his father's, after he had unified Denmark, and that the tradition of such a group was continued under his successors Svein Forkbeard and Canute. In this way one might explain the

Fig. 37 Silver brooch from Ödeshög, Östergötland. Length 8·5 cm.

fresh development in Danish art during the tenth century and the strong connection it seems to have had with Jutland, whence derivatives of it spread to southern Scandinavia. The political conditions are not clear, but there was certainly very strong German influence, and the possibility of an actual occupation cannot be ruled out. Outside Denmark the remains of the Danish kingdom based on York retained a certain independence of law and social organization after its defeat in 954, and contact with it was presumably kept up all the more as conditions in Denmark fell more under German domination.

Plate 51

Plate 59

The striking feature of Danish art in the second half of the tenth century is the strength of the English influence. The silver goblet from the Jellinge mound usually called King Gorm's grave has caused some difficulty, as it may well be a chalice (it has a small figure of a shrine on it), and as it was found with what may be fragments of a paten, a wax candle and a small cross. This makes it seem very unlikely that the grave is that of a heathen king. Though this goblet is considered one of the most representative pieces of Jellinge work, the ornament is poor, in both concept and execution.

Two sets of harness-mount ornaments, from Mammen and Söllested, present an interesting contrast. Those from Mammen resemble the Jellinge bowl in ornament and are the work of a quite insignificant artist. The composition is stiff, and the workmanship careless but showy. The Söllested ornament is

Plates 57, 58

an elegant arrangement of figure-of-eight interlace animals, and instead of the stereotyped cross-hatching of the animal-bodies typical of so much insignificant Jellinge-style work (including the Jellinge bowl and Mammen harness-mounts) the animal-bodies are divided longitudinally by imitation filigree, and the space between this and the body outline on each side is made slightly concave, a delicate device to give some relief to the surface. A similar neat solution is seen in the transformation of the birds' wings into acanthus leaves. The large animal heads at

Fig. 38 Stylised animal ornaments on a silver brooch from Östra Herrestad, Skåne

the ends of the bow illustrate the different approach of the two artists. The Mammen one has a head which might have been taken direct from Continental art with schematically ornamented surfaces. The Söllested one shows a quite different strength, a stylization which stresses the essentials, the large eyes, the ears like cap-peaks, the turned-up snout to expose the long, drama-tically carnivorous teeth. This is what connects the Jellinge style exemplified at Söllested with the earlier Oseberg tradition. Though the grave from which the Söllested harness-mounts come is contemporaneous with that at Mammen from the mid-tenth century, and the ornaments were evidently older when buried than at Mammen, where there were no signs of wear by the reins, it would be wrong to attribute the differences outlined above to difference of date. Just as different artists in the Vest-fold school were more or less gifted, more or less independent, so here we have to do with a difference in merit. The serpentine strip‑animal on the Söllested harness‑mount confirms the evidence of the large animal‑heads: both show a much more lively inheritance of the best of the old Scandinavian tradition. Such details as the way in which the back of the body is widened, or the coupling‑together of the animals by a piece of continuous plait, or the two interlinked bird‑heads on top of the bow, are evidence of this. The maker of the Söllested harness‑mount was from the technical point of view superlatively trained, but was a great artist in addition; he was able to digest such new elements as the palmette and the bird portrait, and assimilate them to the old. The maker of the Mammen ones worked more quickly—one might charitably describe him as an impression‑ist—but was not over‑concerned with quality. His composition was loose, as for example in the clumsily inlaid curving inter‑lace, and he takes in new elements which have caught his fancy. An example of this is a dragon swallowing a man with a bishop (?) watching, which may be meant for Jonah and the whale. He has made no attempt to relate this to the style as a whole.

The Jellinge style has often been regarded as taken directly from Irish art. The foreign influences are more obvious in the worse examples which lack the certainly‑native excellences of the best, and in any case the combination of acanthus leaf with animal ornament and the free‑standing animal‑heads are first found in Irish art in the eleventh century. It is now generally admitted that the Jellinge style developed in the Scandinavian settlements in northern England, though there are still differ‑ences about the dominant influences (Norse? Anglo‑Saxon?)

Fig. 39 and precise locale (Man? The York Kingdom?) concerned. The artist Gaut, whose work in the Isle of Man has already been mentioned (p. 58) was not the inventor of the Jellinge style, which was in any case a matter of gradual evolution. Different views are possible about the stage at which the ex‑

Fig. 39 Animal ornaments on a cross at Kirk Andreas, Isle of Man

periments of such unaccomplished artists as those of the Middle-ton and Gilling Stones can properly be said to have produced a Jellinge style. The Kirk Braddan Cross is an example of the clearly Jellinge style of the Manx crosses. Curiously enough, examples of Jellinge-style work in metal are very rare in England. It may be that it was considered a rather clumsy style, suitable enough on a monumental scale for ceremonial use by half-converted Vikings, but beneath the attention of a skilled English silversmith. In the colonies in Scotland it may have been taken more seriously: the Skail hoard of the mid-tenth century in Orkney has some very good and lively Jellinge ornament on some of the thistle brooches. The sharp angular nature of the interlace and the double lappets on these is typical of what might be called 'insular Jellinge style', distinguishing it from the contemporary art of Scandinavia on the one hand and southern England on the other.

Fig. 40

Fig. 40 Ornament on a thistle brooch from the Skail hoard, Orkney

The style takes its name from the chalice already mentioned, found in the so-called 'King Gorm's mound' at Jellinge, but there is in Jellinge another and more imposing piece of art, Harald Bluetooth's memorial to his ancestors. This is an eight-foot-high, roughly pyramidal granite block, whose erection was epoch-making. The low-relief technique suggests very strongly that it was the work of someone used to working much softer material. Was the sculptor Danish or brought from abroad? It has been said that he was either from northern England, or a Dane from the settlements there who had ac-quired his technique from the sculptors of the Yorkshire crosses. The large Jellinge stone represents something quite new in Scandinavian art but it has a distinct Scandinavian feeling to it, though it represented a dead end and subsequent styles do not seem to be developments of it. This perhaps shows that it derived from elsewhere. The difficulty is that none of the existing stones from the Viking kingdom of York have seemed good enough (with their fundamentally tame Anglian beasts and rather heavy design) to inspire the forceful wild lion at Jellinge. The manuscript art of southern England has resemb-

Plate 60

lances of detail to the plumes on the lion's tail, but no animal portraits of this kind. Some scholars have therefore sought the origin of the Jellinge lion either in the Orient (from which some close, but not of course decisive parallels have been pro-duced) or in Ottonian art. No monument of the period has been so much discussed, and the difficulty in establishing its sources shows merely that its sculptor had sufficient individu-ality to make the work carry his own stamp. He was presum-ably given the main subjects, the memory of Harald's forebears, Harald's deeds and the Christianizing of Denmark and perhaps even the symbolism, of the lion crushing the serpent of evil, and of Christ, which was to be used. The date must have been before 985 (when Harald died) but after his baptism between 953 and 965. If we connect the reference in the inscription about his deeds (which Sune Lindqvist has pointed out was probably added very soon after the original design was com-pleted) with winning all Denmark as a reference to the expul-sion from Hedeby of the German rulers there, then the date can be limited to between 983 and 985. One further reason why it is difficult to establish the affiliations of the Jellinge stone (and other stones of the period) is that most of their real artistic concomitants, the large-scale wood-carvings of the period, have disappeared. The division of the surface by bands tied with loose knots in the corners, and the framing of the inscription, show the affinity with Scandinavian tradition quite clearly; the brooch from Birka for example.

Fig. 41

The next style, named the Mammen style, after a gold-inlaid axe from Bjerringhöj in Jutland, was the result of a new impulse from abroad. Its salient features are a more extensive use of vegetable motifs and greater boldness in their adaptation, and a greater feeling for contrast. The animal bodies or tree trunks are not of constant thickness but become wider and narrower according to the demands of the design, and the interlace around them is of clearly differentiated wiry tentacles. The best products of the new style are the caskets from Cammin and Bamberg and an elk-antler sword-hilt found in Sigtuna. They show by their many new features (the heraldically opposed birds, the lion in profile with head full-face) the eclecticism, based on contacts ranging from England to Kiev, of the year 1000 in Scandinavia. Yet alongside the combat between lion and serpent which was a recognized Christian symbol, we find the frightening masks which represent the native tradition seen already in Oseberg; these were certainly intended to frighten away evil spirits. The runic stone at Skern in Jutland reinforces this by an explicit threat of enchantment on any dis-turber of the dead man's peace. The masks on the stones were garishly coloured, and were by no means empty traditional motifs. Nor need it surprise us to find them accompanied by crosses and pictures of Christ. One might compare the Benty Grange helmet from the early days of the Anglo-Saxon con-version, with its protective Christian cross and pagan boar-image, or the Middleton Cross's blend of Christian and pagan burial-rite. The 15-foot-high stone in Lund has nothing Christian about it. 'Torgisl, son of Esge Björnsson carved the stone to his brothers Olof and Otta, mighty men in the land.' The ornament is of grinning masks and armed wolves: on a group of several stones from Hunnestad, now in Lund, the protective devices range from a cross to a picture of the witch Hyrrokin riding a wolf with snakes as reins.

This brings us up to the year A.D. 1000. To understand the subsequent developments in the art of the Viking Age one has to see them against their historic background. Viking fleets had been harrying the English coast for more than ten years, there was a large settlement of Danes and Norwegians, and in 1017 Canute was chosen king of all England (as he was already of Norway and Denmark). The long-established colonists in the British Isles received a fresh impulse from their homeland. Just as in the previous period the Jellinge style had

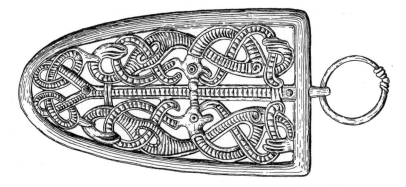

Fig. 41 Bronze brooch from Birka. Length 9·2 cm.

been part of the artistic situation in the North of England, so the traditional feeling for stylization of the Scandinavian artists now developed, on a basically English art, a version of it which was, or became, purely Scandinavian. In Ireland, the Scandi⁄navian defeat at Clontarf in 1014 by no means involved their disappearance. Sigtrygg Silkybeard was to issue coins in Dublin for another twenty years, and the strife between various Irish claimants to the thrones was evidently less destructive than previous harryings. In the cloister there was a new flowering of art, and it is interesting to see how Scandinavian styles either influenced or were adapted by Irish monastic artists.

The most interesting development in Scandinavian art after A.D. 1000 is to be seen in works like the St Paul's Stone and (in spite of Sophus Müller's attribution of the group to Irish influence) the Pseudo⁄Caedmon MS. and the Cambridge University Library Psalter (Ff. I. 23), the latter particularly having been much discussed. Though of mediocre quality, it is important because of its closeness to the Scandinavian tradi⁄tion. Its ornament is a mixture of the acanthus and dragon⁄heads of the Winchester school and Scandinavian features such as the treatment of the leaf as one or two elongated lappets with

Plates 32, 33, 34

upturned points, palmette-loops and elongated animal heads with a drop-shaped eye with its point forwards. The artist may have been a Scandinavian working in an English scriptorium. The ornament in the corners of the St Paul's Stone, the palmette-loop, is in this shape foreign to English art and first appears comparatively late in Irish art; it can be found in Scandinavia in the tenth century. It is presumably based on the oriental palmette ornament. However, the essential feature is not a question of decorative motifs (which are in the main English) but a certain sort of stylization of them. The name Ringerike style which this development has received is a confusion. The accepted use of the term is for the Norwegian material which corresponds to the Mammen style in Denmark, and the name is taken from the red sandstone from Hole in Ringerike in south-eastern Norway which was used for a series of monuments of widely varying styles widely distributed in Norway, in Hallingdal, Toten, Hadeland and Ringerike itself. As far as the vegetable ornament is concerned, Ringerike is simply one facet of the Mammen style. The trees with crossing trunks on the Mammen axe are repeated in the ornament of the stones from Vang and Alstad, and serve to link the Ringerike group with the Cammin casket and the stone from the Guildhall Museum. The stones include realistic pictorial scenes, some native (a scene from the story of Sigurd the killer of Fafnir at Alstad), some introduced from abroad (the Three Wise Men at the manger on the Dynna stone).

A comparison between the famous golden vanes from Hæggen in Norway, and those from Källunge in Gotland and Söderala in Hälsingland, and also the fragments from Denmark and Winchester, shows very clearly the difficulties of tracing the more or less local Scandinavian styles at this date. A sixth from Grimsta, outside Stockholm, is quite different in form, and is perhaps a Slavonic standard; but all the others though so widely separated in place are identical not only in shape, a triangle with one side curved, but in motif (often the conflict between the great beast and the serpent seen on the Jellinge Stone and the St Paul's Stone), and even in execution (by punching, the background being stamped with small circles and the bodies left blank). The Söderala vane is done in pierced work, but shares the small animal, cast in two halves, erect on the point of the vane. This identity makes it tempting to consider all these as the products of one and the same occasion (perhaps Canute's fleet for the invasion of England, in which ships from all over the North took part). Yet from a purely stylistic view they are clearly distinguishable. The Hæggen one is the best; its large bird is surrounded by an oriental-looking border of palmettes, and the acanthus is severely stylized, so that it might well be included in the Ringerike group. The Källunge vane has on one side an acanthus which is more luxuriant, on the other a more stylized one, as well as a tree-motif reminiscent of the Mammen axe; the Söderala artist has the same mixture of both types of acan- thus, and in style his work resembles most the rune-stones of eastern Sweden. The animal on his vane, unlike the others, is turned in to face the mast, and this has presented a difficulty which he has not quite overcome in compelling the figures into a double loop. One can pick out particular features from any of the three, and compare them with English, Ottonian or Oriental art, but one cannot find anything which can be com- pared as a whole, and the group represents a specifically Scan- dinavian version of those common themes (such as the acan- thus) which it uses.

Plate 64

In the tenth century, eastern Sweden had made little con- tribution to Scandinavian art as far as can be seen from surviving material, but in the eleventh a new native style, the Rune-stone style, was created in Gotland and Uppland, the areas where the Vendel style three hundred years earlier had reached its peak. Many of the three thousand stones are signed by their makers; they are the earliest artists in the North to escape anonymity, with the possible exception of Hlewagastir of the Gallehus horn; Gaut worked in the British Isles. The development of the style, the most highly personal and elegant of the Viking Age, can easily be followed in this wealth of material. The style has clear links with Denmark and the ornament is very simple, often only the animal-head which ends the band of the runic inscription. Sometimes we find scenes like those from the Sigurd legend at Ramsund near Eskilstuna, but the main purpose of the stone was its memorial inscription and the ornament was incidental to this. In Gotland there had been an earlier tradition of pictorial stones as monuments (without any inscription) and when people began to erect runic memorials it was natural to incorporate the inscription in the narrative pictorial tradition, even keeping the characteristic mushroomshaped stone of the earlier tradition. But in general the style depended upon a feeling for the rhythmic unadorned curves of the inscription. The basic figure-of-eight patterns and, even more, the minor details of eyes and barbels are of course common to all the Viking styles, but the disciplined clarity of their

Plates 61, 63   arrangement should be recognized as an independent achievement of this school. It might vary in the work of the same artist when he was working for clients of different tastes, ornate or simple, but a recognizable character remains.

One of the first to achieve an individual style was Asmund Kareson, active before the middle of the eleventh century, mainly between Uppsala and Stockholm, but perhaps trained in England to judge from his use of English models. From the same district we have the work of his two younger contemporaries, Fot and Olev; from further west, Livsten, and Tidkume and Balle, working in Västmanland and south-west Uppland and Södermanland. The most confident and elegant virtuoso in the style was Fot; the last of the great artists, Öpir, in whom the original force and springiness of design has been largely replaced by virtuosity. Here as always we must remember that much of the art of which these stones were a part has vanished, leaving only a few examples on small metal objects to which these styles did not properly belong. The rather later Urnes stave church in Norway (after which western versions of the style are often called), Hemse in Gotland and fragments from Brågarp in Skåne, and Hjörring, Denmark give a hint of what there was in large scale wood-carving, and how widespread the style really was. The erection of runic stones was confined in the eleventh century to a small part of the whole area, and has thus perhaps left us with a falsely limited idea of the style's distribution; but it is significant that metal objects in the style are found all over the area the Scandinavian peoples reached.

Plate 62

Urnes with its incredibly elegant, inches-high relief and consequent shadows, its slim animals and convoluted dragons, is the last stage of Scandinavian animal art. One can see that Romanesque is not far away, and though reminiscences of Viking art crop up in later folk art, it had played out its role, and no longer competed with the victorious common European Romanesque.

Select Bibliography

Much of the material used in this volume is taken from short papers published in journals; unfortunately only the principal books and papers can be listed here.

General

BRØNDSTED, J., *The Vikings*. London, 1960.

KENDRICK, T. D., *A History of the Vikings*. London, 1930.

STEENSTRUP, J., *Normannerne*. I–IV. Copenhagen, 1876–82.

Scandinavia

ARBMAN, H., *Birka. Untersuchungen und Studien*. Vol. I. Stockholm, 1940–3.

BAEKSTED, A., *Målruner og troldruner. Runemagiske studier* (with an English summary). Copenhagen, 1952.

BLINDHEIM, CHARLOTTE, 'The Market Place in Skiringsal.' *Acta Archaeologica*, Vol. XXXI. Copenhagen, 1960.

BRÖGGER, A. W., FALK, Hj., GRIEG, S., and SHETELIG, H., *Oseberg-funnet*, Vol. I–IV. Christiania (Oslo), 1917–28.

BRÖGGER, A. W., and SHETELIG, H., *The Viking Ships, Their Ancestry and Evolution* (translated by Kathrine John). Stanford, 1953.

BRØNDSTED, J., 'Danish Inhumation Graves of the Viking Age.' *Acta Archaeologica*, Vol. XXI. Copenhagen, 1936.

DYGGVE, E., 'Gorm's Temple and Harald's Stave-Church.' *Acta Archaeologica*, Vol. XXV. Copenhagen, 1954.

GEIJER, A., *Birka III. Die Textilfunde aus den Gräbern.* Stockholm, 1938.

GRIEG, S., 'Gjermundbufunnet.' *Norske Oldfund VIII.* Oslo, 1947.

HOLMQVIST, W. *Excavations at Helgö, I.* Stockholm, 1961.

HOUGEN, B., 'Osebergsfunnets billedvev.' *Viking,* Vol. IV. Oslo, 1940.

JANKUHN, H., *Die Wehranlagen der Wikingerzeit zwischen Schlei und Treene.* Neumünster, 1937.

JANKUHN, H., *Haithabu, ein Handelsplatz der Wikingerzeit.* Neumünster, 1956.

LINDQVIST, S., *Gotlands Bildsteine,* I–II. 1941–2.

NØRLUND, P., 'Trelleborg.' *Nordiske Fortidsminder* IV⁄1 (with an English summary). Copenhagen, 1948.

PAULSEN, P., *Axt und Kreuz bei den Nordgermanen.* Berlin, 1956.

PETERSEN, J., 'De norske vikingesverd.' *Videnskaps⁄selskapets skrifter,* II, Hist.⁄filos. klasse no. I. Oslo, 1919.

PETERSEN, J., *Vikingetidens smykker.* Stavanger, 1928.

PETERSEN, J., 'Vikingetidens redskaper.' *Skrifter utgitt av Det norske Videnskaps⁄Akademi i Oslo,* II, Hist.⁄filos. klasse no. 4. Oslo, 1951.

RAMSKOU, TH., 'Viking Age Cremation Graves in Denmark.' *Acta Archaeologica,* Vol. XXI. Copenhagen, 1950.

RAMSKOU, TH., 'Lindholm. Preliminary Report.' *Acta Archaeologica,* Vol. XXIV, XXVI, XXVII. Copenhagen, 1953, 1955, 1957.

SELLING, D., *Wikingerzeitliche und frühmittelalterliche Keramik in Schweden.* Stockholm, 1955.

STENBERGER, M., *Die Schatzfunde Gotlands der Wikingerzeit*, I–II. Stockholm, 1947-58.

The British Islands and the Atlantic

A very important periodical for this area is *The Saga Book of the Viking Society* which contains a number of papers on the various aspects and problems.

BLAIR, P. H., *An Introduction to Anglo-Saxon England*. Cambridge, 1956.

BRØGGER, A. W., *Ancient Emigrants*. Oxford, 1928.

BRØNDSTED, J., 'Norsemen in North America before Columbus.' *Smithsonian Institution, An. Rep.*, 1953. Washington, 1954.

COLLINGWOOD, W. S., *Scandinavian Britain*. London, 1908.

DUCKET, E. S., *Alfred the Great*. London, 1957.

STENBERGER, M., ed., *Forntid gårdar i Island*. Copenhagen, 1943.

EKWALL, E., 'The Scandinavian Settlement.' *Historical Geography of England*, ed. H. C. Darby. 1936.

ELDJARN, K., *Kuml og Haugfé*. Akureyri, 1956.

HAMILTON, J. R. C., *Excavations at Jarslhof, Shetland*, Edinburgh, 1956.

MAWER, A., 'The Scandinavian Settlement in England as reflected in English place names.' *Acta Phil. Scand.* 7. 1932.

MEGAW, B. R. S., and E., 'The Norse Heritage in the Isle of Man.' *Chadwick Memorial Studies*. Cambridge, 1950.

NØRLUND, P., *Viking Settlers in Greenland and their descendants during five hundred years*. Cambridge, 1936.

NØRLUND, P., and STENBERGER, M., *Brattahlid. Researches into Norse culture in Greenland.* Copenhagen, 1934.

DE PAOR, M. and L., *Early Christian Ireland.* London, 1958.

SHETELIG, H., ed., *Viking Antiquities in Great Britain and Ireland,* I–IV. Oslo, 1940–54.

STENTON, F. M., *Anglo-Saxon England.* Oxford, 1943.

WALSH, A., *Scandinavian Relations with Ireland during the Viking Period.* Dublin, 1922.

WHEELER, R. E. M., *London and the Vikings.* London, 1927.

WHITELOCK, D., *English Historical Documents,* Vol. I, 500-1042 A.D. London, 1955. (This also contains the Anglo-Saxon Chronicle.)

WILSON, D. M., *The Anglo Saxons.* London, 1960.

Western Europe

ARBMAN, H., *Schweden und das Karolingische Reich.* Stockholm, 1937.

ADIGARD DES GAUTRIES, J., *Les noms de personnes Scandinaves en Normandie de 911 a 1066.* Lund, 1954.

JANKUHN, H., *Haithabu. Ein Handelsplatz der Wikingerzeit.* Neumünster, 1956.

JORANSON, E., *The Danegeld in France.* Rock Island, Illinois, 1924.

LOT, F., 'Les Tributs aux Normands et l'Eglise de France au IXᵉ siecle.' *Bibl. Ec. Chartes,* Vol. LXXXV. 1924.

The Vikings

MUSSET, L., 'Pour l'étude des relations entre les colonies scandinaves d'Angleterre et de Normandie.' *Melanges Fernand Mosse in memoriam.* Paris, 1959.

VOGEL, W., *Die Normannen und das fränkische Reich bis zur Gründung der Normandie.* Heidelberg, 1906.

The Mediterranean

ALLEN, W. E. D., 'The Poet and the Spae-Wife.' *Saga-Book of the Viking Club,* Vol. XV, 3. 1960.

LÉVI-PROVENCAL, E., *Histoire de l'Espagne Musulmane,* I. Paris, 1950.

MELVINGER, A., *Les Premières Incursions des Vikings en Occident d'après les Sources Arabes.* Uppsala, 1955.

STEFANSSON, J., 'The Vikings in Spain from Arabic (Moorish) and Spanish Sources.' *Saga Book of the Viking Club,* Vol. VI. 1909.

The East

Most of the modern Russian literature on this subject is to be found in short papers in the journal *Sovetskaya Arkheologiya* and in the series *Materialy i Issledovaniya Arkheologii SSSR.* However, these do not usually contain summaries in non-slavonic languages.

ARNE, T. J., *La Suède et l'Orient.* Uppsala, 1914.

CROSS, S., *The Russian Primary Chronicle.* Harvard, 1930.

DUNLOP, D. M., *The History of the Jewish Khazars.* Princeton, 1954.

FALK, K. O., *Dnjeprforsarnas namn i kejsar Konstantin Porphyrogennetos De Administrando Imperio.* Lund, 1951.

LINDER-WELIN, S. U., 'Wasit the Mint Town.' *Meddelanden från Lunds univ. hist. museum*, 1955.

PASZKIEWICZ, H., *The Origin of Russia.* London, 1954.

THOMSEN, V., *The Relations between Ancient Russia and Scandinavia and the Origin of the Russian State.* Oxford, 1866.

RAUDONIKAS, W. J., *Die Norrmannen der Wikingerzeit und das Lado-gagebiet.* Stockholm, 1930.

STENDER-PETERSEN, A., *Varangica.* Aarhus, 1953.

ZEKI VALIDI TOGAN, A., *Ibn Fadlan's Reisebericht.* Leipzig, 1939.

Viking Art

ALMGREN, B., *Bronsnycklar och djurornamentik.* Uppsala, 1955.

BRØNDSTED, J., *Early English Ornament.* London, 1924.

HOLMQVIST, W., 'Viking Art in the Eleventh Century.' *Acta Archae-ologica*, Vol. XXXII. Copenhagen, 1951.

KENDRICK, T. D., *Late Saxon and Viking Art.* London, 1949.

KENDRICK, T. D., *Anglo-Saxon Art to 900 A.D.* London, 1938.

KERMODE, P., *Manx Crosses.* London, 1907.

SHETELIG, H., *Osebergfunnet*, Vol. III. Christiania (Oslo), 1920.

SHETELIG, H., 'The Norse Style of Ornamentation in the Viking Settlements.' *Acta Archaeologica*, Vol. XIX. Copenhagen, 1948.

Sources of Illustrations

Grateful acknowledgements for the plates are made to the following individuals and institutions: Statens Historiska Museum, Stockholm: 1–5, 8–10, 12–17, 21, 22, 42, 43, 52, 53, 55, 56, 61, 63, 64, 66; National Museum Copenhagen: 6–7, 11, 24, 44, 59, 60; Holger Arbman: 18, 36–39, 50, 57, 58, 65, 67; Sverre Marstrander, Keeper of Anti-quities, Trondheim: 19; Viking Ship Museum, Oslo: 20, 45–49; Universitets Oldsaksamling, Oslo; 25, 62; J. V. S. Megaw, courtesy the Russell Trust, University of Edinburgh: 27; The Yorkshire Museum, York: 28; A. L. Binns: 29, 30; Trustees of the British Museum: 31, 35; Guildhall Museum, London: 32; University Library, Cambridge: 34; Bodleian Library, Oxford: 33; University Museum, Lund: 51, 54. The majority of the figures have been drawn by Bertil Centerwall, Lund: (figs. 21–24, 26, 30, 33–35, 39 after H. Shetelig; fig. 19 from a photograph from the State Hermitage, Leningrad; figs. 31, 32 after Nicolaysen; fig. 40 after J. Anderson). The remainder have been re-drawn or come from the following sources: figs. 1, 4: M. E. Weaver after H. Arbman; fig. 2: P. P. Pratt after H. Jankuhn; fig. 3: P. P. Pratt and W. Dodd; fig. 5: M. E. Weaver after C. Blindheim; fig. 6: M. E. Weaver after A. Sorrell; figs. 7, 8: M. E. Weaver after Ham-ilton; fig. 10: P. P. Pratt after T. A. Dallman; figs. 11, 12: P. P. Pratt; fig. 13: M. E. Weaver; fig. 16: A. Falkenhovf, Lund; fig. 18: P. P. Pratt after Artsikovski; figs. 25: H. Shetelig, *Osebergfunnet* Vol. III, fig. 78 (1920); The maps have been drawn by Shalom Schotten (fig. 9 after T. D. Kendrick; fig. 15 after H. Jankuhn) and Diana Holmes.

PLATES

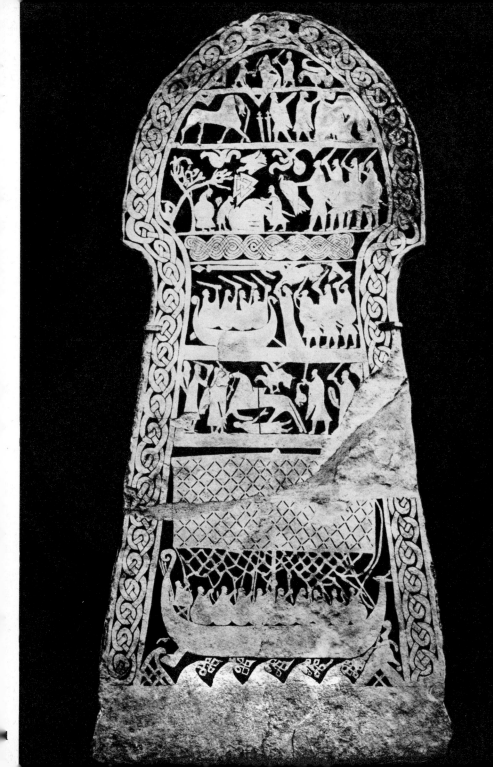

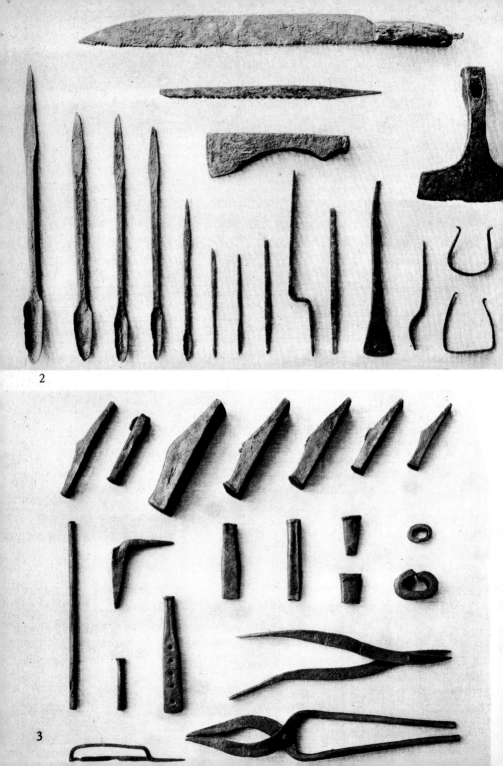

2

3

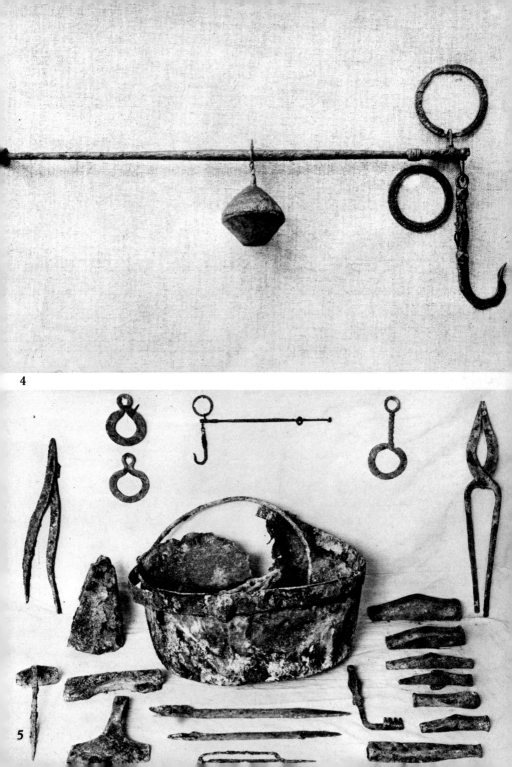

4

5

6

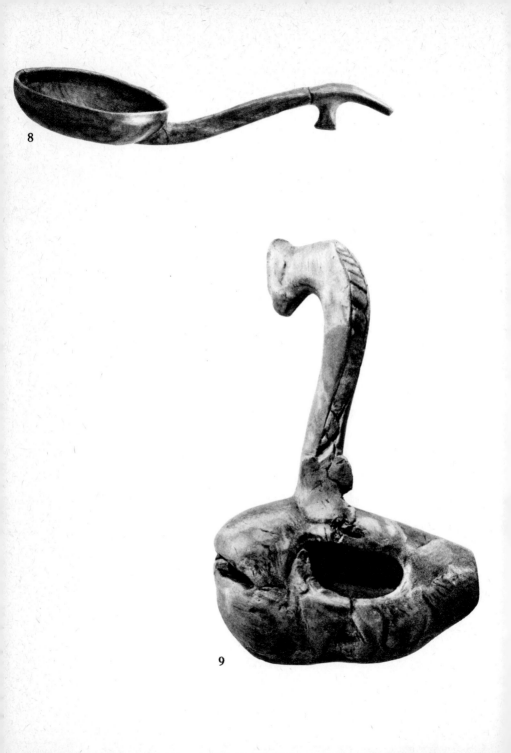

8

9

12

13

14

15

16

17

18

19

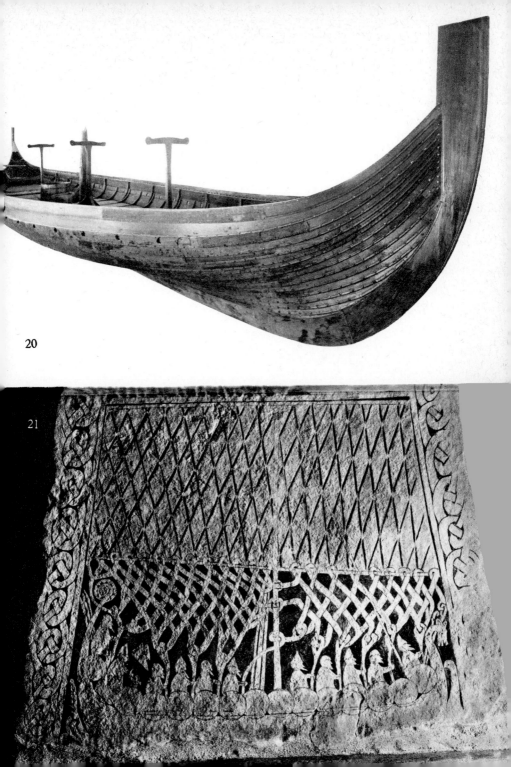

20

21

23

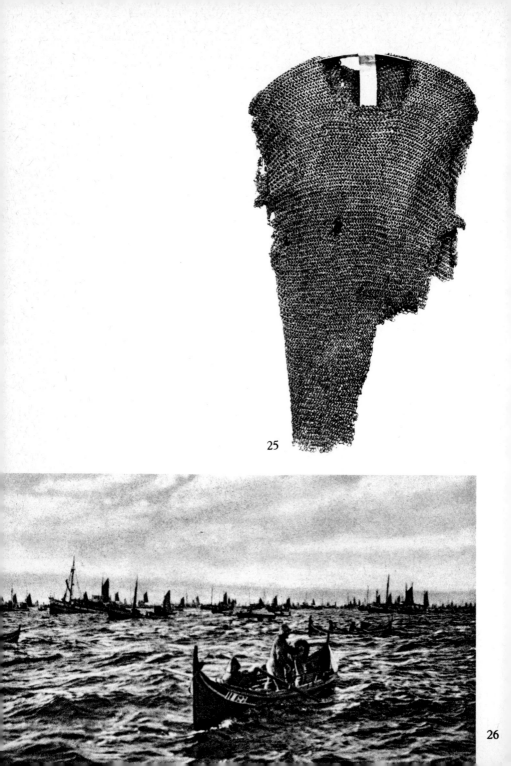

25

26

27

28

31

32

36

37

38   39

40

41

42

3

45

46

47

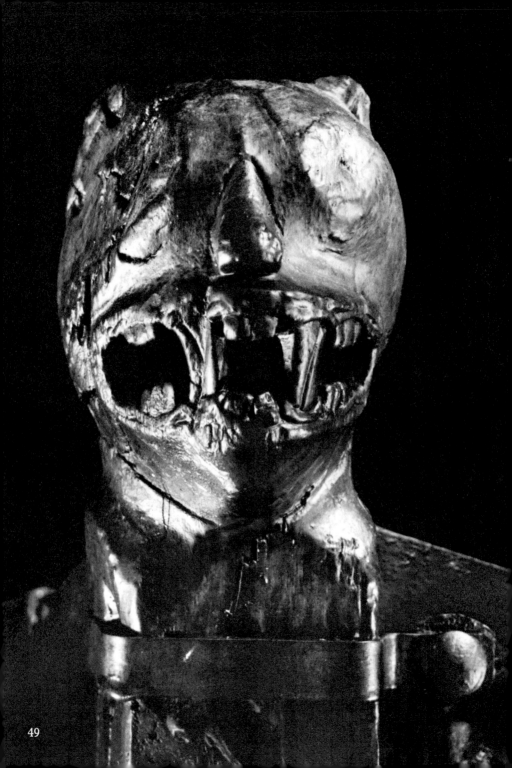

49

50

51

52

53

54

55

56

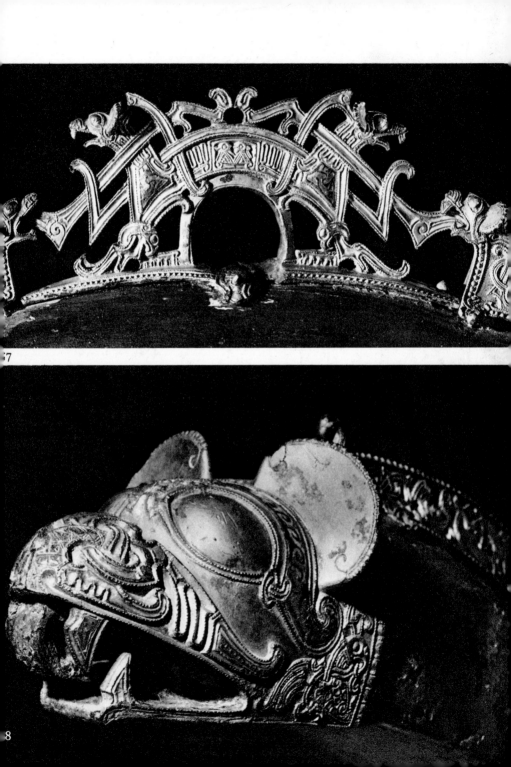

62

63

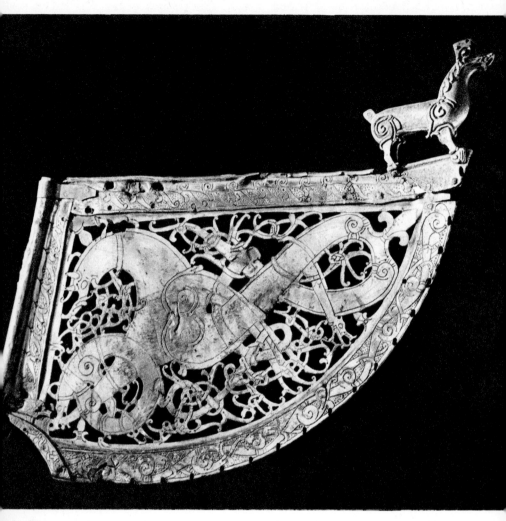

64

Notes on the Plates

It should be emphasized that the dates given in these notes are intended only as a general indication for the reader.

1   Memorial stone at Stora Hammar, Lärbro, Gotland. Apparently repre, senting scenes from a heroic poem of which only some passages are known in the Icelandic scald Bragai's *Ragnarsdrapa*. The hero, Hild, is abducted leaving his family to seek revenge. Like most of the Gotlandic stones this one has no runic inscription and there is little chance of inter, preting the figures. Height 3·5 m. Late eighth century.

2, 3, 5   Tools from a craftsman's chest found in the dried-up Lake Mäster, myr, Gotland. The chest contained about 150 tools, showing that the owner was a wandering craftsman and jack-of-all-trades—smith, joiner, carpenter and kettle-mender. About A.D. 1000. Statens Historiska Museum, Stockholm.

4   The steelyard balance from the same find at Mästermyr. Length 35·3 cm.

6   Excavation at Lindholm near Aalborg, Denmark. The high narrow ploughed ridges mark the original surface of the fields of the Viking period. The boat-shaped stone outlines at the bottom left are cremation graves. Some are incomplete as stones appear to have been taken from them to make later graves.

7   The ship grave at Ladby, Fyn, Denmark. The anchor and chain cable can be seen in the foreground. The floor is comparatively flat and the hull shallow (though only the lower strakes of the hull are shown). Tenth century.

8, 9, 10   Domestic implements of birchwood from the Årby boat burial, Uppland. Tenth century. (8) Spoon with a keel on the underside of the handle which makes it possible to stand the spoon horizontally on a table. Length 19·6 cm. (9) Curved ladle of an unusual type. Length 19·2 cm. (10) A scoop similar to those used today in northern Sweden

197

as drinking vessels. Greatest width 11·2 cm. Statens Historiska Museum, Stockholm.

11 Twelve axes from Gjerrild near Grenaa, Jutland. They are threaded onto a stave made of spruce, a tree which did not grow in Denmark during the Viking Age, and it must have come as part of the original export packing from Norway or Sweden. Length of the stave 73 cm. Ninth-tenth century. National Museum, Copenhagen.

12 Silver pendant cross from Birka, with filigree ornamentation. In the centre is a rock crystal with an engraved sign on its back. Late Carolingian or Ottonian. Length 4·7 cm. Ninth century. Statens Historiska Museum, Stockholm.

13 Silver-gilt pendant cross from Birka with filigree and repoussé ornament. This is the oldest known crucifix made in Scandinavia. Length 4·7 cm. About 900. Statens Historiska Museum, Stockholm.

14 Bucket of birchwood found at Birka, covered with a thin bronze sheet and decorated with engraved birds, trees and scrolls. Imported from Northumbria or Scotland. Eighth century or beginning of ninth century. Height 18·3 cm. Statens Historiska Museum, Stockholm.

15 Birka, showing the interior of the fort, with the town (in the 'Black Earth' belt) in the background.

16 Glass pieces from a game. Nine in dark-green glass and seventeen in a light blue-green, with centre a 'king' with dark-blue facial features, a 'crown' and decorative threads round the body. Found at Birka, probably Oriental. Diameter 2·5–2·7 cm. Ninth century. Statens Historiska Museum, Stockholm.

17 Glass beakers and pottery imported from the mouth of Rhine. The large jug in the centre has a pattern inlaid with tin (it is of a type known as Tatting ware). To the right a stone with a runic inscription. All from Birka. Height of the jug 24·7 cm. Statens Historiska Museum, Stockholm.

18 A view of Kaupang, Skiringsal, Norway. The site of the market town lies in the foreground.

19 A Norwegian grave mound, Herlaugshaugen, Trøndelag.

20 Gokstad ship. The side rudder and thwartships tiller can be seen just above the shields. The small slit cut at the top of the round rowing, ports allowed the blade of the oar to be passed through from inside. As the top of the prow and the stern projected above the protective layer of blue clay in the grave mound they were not preserved. The Viking Ship Museum, Oslo.

21 Ship on a figured stone from Smiss, Stenkyrka, Gotland. The stern ornament is reminiscent of that from the Ile de Groix. The interlace below the sail perhaps represents a decorative development of an arrange, ment of multiple sheets which would hold the sail more efficiently. At the mast-head is a weather-vane. About 800. Visby, Gotlands Fornsal.

22 Sparlösa runic stone, Västergötland. The figures are partly executed in low relief, a technique which is very rare in the Viking Period. The house shown at the top is of the same type as on the Birka coins. About 800.

23 A traditional long-house on the Mainland of Shetland which may be compared with the reconstruction of Jarlshof, fig. 6.

24 Trelleborg, Zealand, Denmark. This aerial view shows clearly the plan of the military camp with the inner four squares of long-houses with slightly curved walls surrounded by a circular wall. In the outer camp are thirteen long-houses of similar design but on a smaller scale, and two others set parallel to one another. To the south-west are the exterior defen, sive works. Probably a camp for the troops of the Danish kings. About 1000.

25 Mailshirt found in the mound 'Jarlshaug', Trøndelag, Norway in about 1750. Finds of mailshirts are very rare in the Viking graves. Probably Viking or early Medieval. Universitets Oldsaksamling, Oslo.

26 This view of the herring fleet of the nineteen hundreds at Lofoten gives some impression of a scene that must have been common in the Viking Period. Two rowing boats in the foreground, though much smaller than their predecessors, have preserved the traditional shape of the hull.

27 Stone from Iona, showing what appears to be a Viking ship.

The Vikings

28 Bronze chape of a sword scabbard found at York. The pattern is of an animal and serpent interlaced in the Jellinge style. Length 9 cm. Tenth century. Yorkshire Museum, York.

29 Cross from Middleton, Yorkshire. It shows the characteristic furnishing of a pagan Viking grave. The shape between the spear on the left and the pointed helmet may perhaps be a bird. The shield, sword and axe are to the right, and the sax or long knife is laid across the body. Mid-tenth century.

30 The reverse side of the same cross shows a typically crude and schematic version of the so-called English Jellinge style. Length of the panel 70 cm.

31 Page from the Liber Vitae of New Minister at Winchester showing King Canute and his wife, Aelfigvu-Emma, placing a golden cross on the altar of the Minster. This book is a register and martyrology of 1016–1020. British Museum, MS. Stowe 944.

32 Stone from Old St Paul's churchyard. It represents the animal style of Canute's day, and contains Scandinavian elements of the Ringerike style. Guildhall Museum, London.

33 Design for a binding in the Caedmon manuscript. On the face is an English acanthus pattern and on the spine, a Ringerike ornament. 1030–50. Bodleian Library, MS. Junius 11, Oxford.

34 Initial formed of a dragon with Scandinavian features in the same manu-script as the typical Winchester style. Early eleventh century. University Library, MS. Ff. I, 23, Cambridge.

35 Selection of Viking silver pennies (all coins except (1) reproduced same size). (1) Sweden, Birka c. 880 (Enlarged x 2). 2–6 Vikings of north-eastern England c. 895–c. 915: (2) Uncertain mint in Yorkshire c. 895 (imitating penny of Alfred the Great) (3) Uncertain mint south of Humber c. 895 (imitating two pennies of Alfred the Great): (4) York, 'King Siefred' c. 895–900: (5) York 'King Canute' c. 895–900: (6) York 'unknown King' c. 915. 7–11. Hiberno-Norse Kings of York 921–954: (7) Sihtric I Caoch ('Sigtrygg One-Eye'), 921–926: (8) Anlaf II Guthfrithsson. 939–941: (9) Sihtric II Sihtricsson ('Sigtrygg of the Jewels'), c. 942: (10) Ragnvald II Guthfrithson, c. 943: (11) Anlaf I

Sihtricsson ('Anlaf Quaran' or 'Anlaf the Sandal'), Third Reign, 942–952. (12) Eric Blood-axe, York, Second Reign, 952–954. (13) Southern Sweden, (Lund?) c. 975? 14–17 Contemporary Imitations of English Pence, c. 995, Ireland: (14) Sihtric III Anlafsson ('Sigtrygg Silkybeard'), Ireland. Dublin: (15) Olaf Tryggvasson, Norway, uncertain mint: (16) Svein Haraldsson ('Svein Forkbeard'), Denmark: (17) Olaf Skotkonung ('Olaf Tax-King'), Sweden. Coins, 1, 13, 15–17, Statens Historiska Museum, Stockholm; coins 2–12, 14, British Museum.

36 Horse-bit of a type which is often found in Scandinavian tenth-century graves. From the region of Rouen. Musée des Antiquités, Rouen.

37 A pair of Scandinavian tortoise brooches from a woman's grave at Pitres, Normandy. Ninth century, Musée des Antiquités, Rouen.

38 Viking sword found in the river Loire. The hilt is decorated with inlaid silver and copper threads. Ninth century. Musée de Nantes.

39 Viking sword from Sørup, near Løgstør, Jutland. The brass plates are engraved with geometrical designs. Ninth century. Aarhus Museum.

40 Staraja Ladoga (Aldeigjuborg). A view showing the earthen ramparts which have been badly damaged by earlier diggings.

41 Staraja Ladoga. The remains of wooden buildings in the bottom (Finnish?) layer. From Repnikov's excavation in 1913.

42 Silver fragment from a hoard from Öster Ryftes, Fole, Gotland. Probably an arm of a Byzantine or Russian reliquary, with an engraved figure of a saint. Length, 2·9 cm. About 1000. Statens Historiska Museum, Stockholm.

43 Hoard of silver arm rings found at Asarve, Hemse, Gotland. The spiral ones are imported from eastern Europe, perhaps from the Kama region. This is the second largest silver hoard from Gotland, weighing 15 lb. Ninth century. Statens Historiska Museum, Stockholm.

44 Ketilsfjord, Greenland. In the Middle Ages, a monastery was founded below the mountain at the side of the fjord. This photograph gives some idea of the harsh landscapes that the Scandinavians encountered.

45 Oseberg. The Academician's animal-head post, (cf. fig. 45). Length 52 cm. Viking Ship Museum, Oslo.

46 Oseberg. Detail of the Baroque Master's sledge shaft. Viking Ship Museum, Oslo.

47 The Oseberg wagon. The decoration on the side and end of the wagon⁄ body is executed in different styles. Viking Ship Museum, Oslo.

48 Oseberg. Detail of a terminal from one of the supports of the wagon⁄ body. Viking Ship Museum, Oslo.

49 Oseberg. Terminal from one of the corner posts on Shetelig's sledge in the shape of a head. Such heads were clearly meant to seem menacing, and terror was an important element in the artistic effect. Viking Ship Museum, Oslo.

50 Small silver pendant in the form of a man's head from a Viking grave at Aska, Hagebyhöga, Östergötland. The man has a helmet decorated with conventionalized birds. Length 3·5 cm. Tenth century. Statens Historiska Museum, Stockholm.

51 Hilt of a sword found at Dybeck, Skåne. Silver⁄gilt with animal orna⁄ ment of southern English style and inlaid with niello. An English work, or made by a Scandinavian craftsman trained in England. Length of the cross⁄guard, 10·2 cm. About 1000. Statens Historiska Museum, Stockholm.

52, 53 Two silver filigree brooches made by two different techniques from a hoard found at Eketorp, Närke, Sweden. The Jellinge style animal orna⁄ ment shows the influence of the Oseberg artists. Length 8 cm., 7.8 cm. First half of the tenth century. Statens Historiska Museum, Stockholm.

54 Silver⁄gilt pendant in the form of a man (probably an amulet) from the Eketorp hoard. He is dressed in a garment down to the knees, and is holding his sword in both hands. His eyes were apparently inlaid. Length 3·7 cm. Statens Historiska Museum, Stockholm.

55 Detail of a sword pommel from Stora Ihre, Hellvi, Gotland, showing a mixture of old and new features. The central roundel contains a lion with a bird's head: this can be best seen by reversing the picture. About 800. Statens Historiska Museum, Stockholm.

56 Silver brooch, with inlaid niello, from Gärdslösa, Öland. A good exponent of the Borre style. Diameter 8·5 cm. Tenth century. Statens Historiska Museum, Stockholm.

57, 58 Details of a pair of bronze gilt harness mounts from Søllested, Fyn, Denmark. They are decorated with Jellinge style ornament of an exqui/ site quality showing the tradition of older Scandinavian animal orna/ ments. Tenth century, National Museum, Copenhagen.

59 Silver beakers from Denmark. Above, from Fejø: continental but in a style inspired by southern England, partly gilt and inlaid with niello. Height 9·7 cm. About 800. Below left, from Lejre, Zealand: Danish work, partly gilt and with niello inlay. Height 4·5 cm. Tenth century. Below right, from Jellinge; perhaps a chalice. Height 3·8 cm. Tenth century. All in National Museum, Copenhagen.

60 One side of the Jellinge stone, showing the crucifixion scene. Christ is surrounded by interlace, part of the runic inscription can be seen at the bottom of the stone. About 980.

61 Runic rock carving at Sollentuna, Uppland. Mid eleventh century.

62 Detail of the stave church at Urnes. Mid eleventh century.

63 Runic stones at Spelvik, Södermanland. Eleventh century.

64 Bronze/gilt weather vane from Söderala church, Hälsingland. The leaves which originally hung from the holes along the curved underside have been lost. The vane, in an English style, probably comes from a ship in Canute's fleet. Length 44 cm. Statens Historiska Museum, Stockholm.

65 Above: both sides of a reliquary of silver inlaid with niello in a hoard from Valbo, Gästrikland. On one side the Virgin, on the other Saint Nicolas. Diameter 2 cm. Eleventh century. Below: a fragment cut out of a silver object. Probably the head of Christ. In a silver hoard from Valdarve, Eskelhem, Gotland. About 1000. Diameter 1·75 x 1·45 cm.

66 Silver arm/ring from Hejslunds, Havdhem, Gotland. Greatest dia/ meter 9·2 cm. Eleventh century. Statens Historiska Museum, Stock/ holm.

67 The Piraeus Lion which stands at the entrance to the Arsenal, Venice. A marble lion taken by Venetians from the Greek harbour of the Piraeus. It is not in itself a Nordic monument but bears a runic inscription which can just be seen in the darker patch on the shoulder. The inscription is so worn, however, that it cannot be deciphered.

Index